instant enlightenment

Also by the Barefoot Doctor

Liberation
Manifesto
Return of the Urban Warrior
Twisted Fables for Twisted Minds

instant enlightenment

108 blessings

BAREFOOT DOCTOR

Element
An Imprint of HarperCollins*Publishers*
77–85 Fulham Palace Road,
Hammersmith, London W6 8JB

The website address is: www.thorsonselement.com

-☼- element ™

and *Element* are trademarks of
HarperCollins*Publishers* Ltd

First published 2004

10 9 8 7 6 5 4 3 2 1

Stephen Russell asserts the moral right to be
identified as the author of this work

A catalogue record of this book is
available from the British Library

ISBN 0 00 719094 8

Printed and bound in Great Britain by
Clays Ltd, St Ives plc, Bungay

dedicated …

entirely to you

contents

what instant enlightenment is

Maybe it's about clearing the fog of the everyday by stepping aside momentarily and seeing everything from a new angle – taking your attention off yourself and your personal dramas that are obscuring the clarity within and the magic without, and placing it instead on the energetic/spiritual region of reality. Every time you do this you receive a blessing which you then pass on to others.

Sending a blessing to someone, as I'm doing now for you 108 times, is different from making a wish. A wish is good, but perhaps a bit woolly round the edges. Sending a blessing is also different from praying for someone, as this implies a separation between you, the person you're praying for, and the divine realms, and so is going places that may not fit with a busy, pragmatic lifestyle. It's also different from doing an affirmation, which is powerful for getting what you want but is necessarily all about you.

When sending a blessing, however – though that blessing may well involve a wish made slick by visualization, and may have been formulated by affirmative thought – something indefinable, ineffable happens, something greater than its constituent parts, which mysteriously instigates a direct link between sender and recipient through the divine realm that connects, directs and protects us all. I give it, you get it, you pass it on, and so on. That's the way this magic circuit works and who knows what healing and amazement will come of it.

The idea of blessing someone or something is to inject them or it with positive energy by the use of thought and intention. The opposite action is to curse someone or something by injecting them or it with negative energy. You don't need a syringe to do either. You don't even need to be in the same room or even on the same continent. Thought travels freely through time and space. Thought with intention behind it always finds its target.

The energy you transmit by thought always returns your way eventually, generally with far more force behind it, having gathered its own momentum after swinging round the universe. Transmit positivity towards people or situations, and positive energy will come back your way, in time, multiplied. Conversely, transmit negativity and that's what you'll get back. There is no neutral position because there is no such thing as neutral energy. It's either negative or positive – yin or yang. If you don't consciously choose to transmit positive energy you will naturally default to transmitting negative energy.

If you accept this, you don't have to be a genius to realize that it's in your best interests to transmit as much positive energy and as little negative energy towards people and situations as you can. In some rare cases, the motivation to make blessings is purely altruistic, but saints are few and far between. So if, as is likely, you're not one yourself, don't punish or berate yourself for it – no one said you had to be a saint. Mostly, however, the impulse behind the motivation is the same as that of someone with a shrewd eye for investment – investing positive energy to gain more positive energy, along with all the ramifications down here on the ground that that implies.

The nature of the impulse doesn't matter – blessings reach their recipients regardless, as well as which, the act of sending a blessing – even when initially inspired by self-interest – instantaneously connects you to the altruistic impulse if only for that moment, and in that moment comes grace – that peculiar energy that only arises in selflessness, which makes the air seem to hum and sparkle all around you and in whose aftermath many wondrous things tend to occur in your life.

However, you have, as have we all – forgive me stating the obvious – felt hurt by life from time to time and have thus, as an unconscious protective reaction, developed a set of negative beliefs, which have inevitably found expression in your thoughts, words, body language and deeds from time to time. You're human. Rarely, though, will all your thoughts, actions and deeds be either totally negative, or, for that matter, totally positive. There'll be a mixture of the two. The key to maintaining a good relationship with your world, which after all is what we're on about here, is to do what you can to remain at least 51 per cent in the black – just as (hopefully) you do with your bank balance – something for which we all need as much reminding as possible. Hence this book – to remind you – and, of course, me – to stay in the black – because no one will, or can, bail you out if you don't.

And what right have I to remind you by sending you these 108 blessings that you, in turn, might send them on and thus receive the benefits? Same right as you or anyone else.

In fact, each blessing was inspired by the themes of pieces posted daily on my website which elicited the greatest amount of positive public feedback. Hence I know they have the greatest value and resonance (which in itself still gives me no more or less of a right to transmit blessings than anyone else, but certainly gives me encouragement to go ahead regardless). And why would I want to do such a thing (apart from the obvious reasons stated above)? Because it will be gratifying watching the world's atmosphere change for the better when enough people start flinging the blessings about the place and people everywhere start feeling the actual results in their lives – and I love gratification, as I'm sure you do too.

But why, other than attracting a substantial increase of positive energy and the effects of that into your life, and enjoying the gratification of having helped the world heal itself, would you want to get involved with this book?

Why not?

Do you have any better games to play today (or tonight)?

Talking of games, I'd like very much to thank and acknowledge my beloved and intrepid PA, Naked Nurse, aka Carrie Montgomery, bless her heart, for all her incredible help in preventing this game we're about to play from having ended up as merely a useless pile of crumpled notes on the floor of my office.

the deeper significance of the number 108 (and why not 109?)

All three major spiritual paths of the East – Hinduism, Buddhism and Taoism – (these, especially the latter, incidentally, having formed the bedrock of my own spiritual training) imbue the number 108 with special power. Now you may always or sometimes, depending on your life-phase, mood and company, maintain that numerology belongs under the umbrella of superstition, and you could be right. But if you go with the fundamental assertion, (as do serious followers of the esoteric, hence authentic, aspects of the paths above, as well as those who adhere to western spiritual paths) that you create your own experience of reality according to which set of beliefs you've managed to install on your hard drive – in other words, by what you do with your mind at the deepest level – you could safely assert that by believing a number has power, it has. As you see it, so it will be.

And if you're not willing to entertain that possibility, there's really not much point reading this book – sure, buy it for a friend who's into things like this, but don't waste time reading or trying to use it yourself because the very idea of a blessing – or curse for that matter – having any actual effect, rests largely on this premise – largely, but by no means exclusively, as there's more to this, in the deeper mystical sense, than you or I understand.

On the other hand, if you swing between the two positions, as most of us do most of the time, it really doesn't matter anyway – it's only a number. I could have made it 109 blessings – but I didn't. The blessings themselves are still the blessings and that's what counts (excuse my proclivity towards the pointless pun).

For me, though, it's always had appealing significance, the number 108, introduced as I was to the esoteric ways of the East at an early age. I've always found it warming somehow that Buddhist rosaries have 108 beads, the reciting of sacred mantras repeated 108 times with the thumb-and-fingering past of each successive bead to counteract the 108 weaknesses with the 108 strengths, or that a large bell is rung 108 times at the beginning of each year for good fortune, or that there are, according to Buddhist mythology, 108 bodhisattvas (beings aspiring to and in training for Buddhahood, who, having actually achieved enlightenment and freedom from rebirth on this crazy old planet, choose instead to keep reincarnating, until each and every one of us has finally achieved liberation from all suffering – pissing in the wind perhaps, but 108 blessings on them and all of us for giving it a bash).

Further, in Taoist numerology the number 9 carries the creative, generative impulse more strongly than any other prime number. Multiply that by 12 (to make 108) and you have at your disposal, if you go with the theory, enough creative, generative impulse to reach all aspects of the body, as expressed in the energy flow within the 12 meridians, and to reach all aspects of the soul, as expressed in the 12 sets of animal characteristics, which, between them, describe the full range of human expression and even all aspects of the universe itself, as expressed by the 12 signs of the zodiac.

And I could go on about how Shiva, Vishnu and even the Buddha each have 108 aliases, how the Tibetan Buddhists' legends of Shambalah, the mystical paradise, tell of 108 enlightened, immortal, resident masters (or mistresses) there, or even about how Sid The Barber of Commercial Road was at number 108, but I think you take my point – with all those billions of minds over the aeons lending their mental power to belief in its sanctity and special talismanic quality, 108 is a number to be reckoned with.

And that's just one reason I didn't make it 109.

what you'll encounter when you read this book

I don't know why I'm telling you this really – you might as well read the book and find out for yourself – but I think it's good manners. It's like phoning you just before we meet up to say I'll be wearing a red suit. Red suit? I just thought I'd let you know in advance. That's actually one of the reasons I don't wear red suits (one of the 108 weaknesses, by the way, wearing red suits), apart from the fact that red doesn't suit me – I'd find it irksome having to phone people every time, ahead of time, to warn them.

That being said, you'll see a headline – something like 'YOU ARE BLESSED WITH FREEDOM' – you'll know it's a headline because it'll be stand-alone and big. Opposite that you'll find what's meant to be, according to the immutable law of Neat and Tidy, which in reality I break many times in both directions, approximately 200 words of text that will take you through a momentary internal process, which sometimes may appear to have nothing directly to do with the concept of, say, freedom, using the above example, and which will usually involve the idea of you transmitting positive energy towards others, quite often in the form of visualizing world peace and abundance for all, as nothing brings good energy back your way quite as strongly.

Sometimes you'll be doing it for real, other times you'll just be going through the motions. It doesn't matter – as long as you keep doing it long enough to catch a few real ones along the way. When you've done, when you've made your internal offering, you'll be told, using the above example, 'You are now blessed with freedom.' Don't bother arguing with this – it's for your own good, after all – simply accept the blessing as well as you can – over time it gets easier.

Incidentally, there is nothing numerologically significant about the number 200 – it's just the amount allotted me per page by my publishers for purposes of design. Also, there is no need to restrict yourself to reading or using the book in a linear fashion – let it fall open where it will, if you will – no one blessing is any more significant than any other. Yes, the shape of freedom in a blessing might look different to the shape of, say, integrity, and perhaps seem momentarily more significant to you, but fundamentally, when you look deep enough, all 108 blessings eventually lead to, and form part of, the whole of one big meta-blessing comprised of 108 aspects – the ineffable, the Tao, the Great Mother of all existence and non-existence – that underlying, invisible, meta–conscious, intelligent, benign, *a priori*, generative force, whose imprint and pattern creates, animates, permeates, informs, envelops, connects and ultimately directs, all known and unknown phenomena throughout the entirety of both existence and non-existence, experience of which, even for one fleeting moment, no other blessing can even think of matching.

But come on, let's do the blessings now, let's cut to the main attraction ...

... so, sit back, loosen your tie, adjust your décolletage, kick off your slippers or low sling-back heels, shuffle about in the chair or wherever you are, get comfortable and the transmission will begin.

start of transmission

(I am now actually sending you immense waves of pure love, contained not just within the meaning and structure of the words, phrases, sentences, paragraphs and pages themselves but also in the spaces between the letters in the words and in the gaps between the sentences and paragraphs, even in those small spaces between a comma and the next word – every space is filled with love.

Be open to receive it. Then pass it on – in your own time. Thank you. At ease.)

instant enlightenment — 1

You are blessed with the power
to create the rest of your life
from scratch

Picture yourself walking along an enchanted pathway in a vast magic garden. Bordering the path on either side is lush foliage growing higher than your head, with brightly coloured flowers of such intense vividness it makes you blink. Birds are singing to each other and you're so attuned you can understand their song. At the end of the pathway you notice a large arch beyond which seems to be a meadow, but the air there is shimmering so it's hard to tell – it could just be empty space. As you approach the arch you notice an inscription carved into it, reading: 'As you pass beneath this arch you leave your past behind and enter an entirely new reality, where you can create whatever you want.'

So you stride boldly through and there, on the other side, you find absolutely nothing. Not nothing in the boring sense of nothing to play with, but nothing in the sense of complete emptiness. You have entered the void. Yet rather than it feeling scary, it feels incredibly warm and embracing. Then, without any words actually being spoken, you hear a voice inside you saying, 'Create the rest of your life from scratch.'

So you relax and pretty soon find images flooding your mind – images of qualities you want to access and develop, images of you looking immensely contented, healthy, fulfilled, exhilarated and at peace. And as they get clearer, you find yourself feeling ever more relaxed until you suddenly notice, as if waking from a dream, that everything you've been picturing is actually all around you in reality.

You are now blessed with the power to create the rest of your life from scratch.

instant enlightenment —2—

*You are blessed with
unrestricted access to the
adventure of life*

It's time to cut loose of all inner restrictions now and live the adventure as large as you can possibly manage. Liberate yourself from the suffering of stifling self-imposed restraints for evermore, and the adventure is yours for the taking now.

Of course this will bring pain, the pain of letting go of structures you've created internally and externally that no longer serve you. The pain of ripping off a plaster hitherto adhered to the hairy leg of your soul. But after the pain comes first relief, then comfort, then bliss.

Let wane anything in your life that no longer works to help you optimize your enjoyment of each and every moment from now on, and welcome the adventure of the unknown.

You now are blessed with unrestricted access to the adventure of life.

instant enlightenment 3

You are blessed with the
ineffable miracle of your own
existence

When you find yourself pushing too hard for things to work out and it's causing you to tense up, stop for a moment – long enough to read this – and become aware of your physical situation: how you're holding your body, how your shoulders and upper back are straining, your lower back stiffening, your breath is moving irregularly and inflamingly and your thoughts are racing through your brain. Do you like the feeling? If not, slow your breath down. Relax your shoulders, let them drop, soften your upper back, soften your face, relax your belly and your lower back.

Then think of what an ineffable miracle your existence is. Not just as an abstract concept – though it's a fine abstract concept to entertain – but as a real flesh and bones reality here and now in this present moment. Anything more than that – your plans working out, for instance – is a bonus.

Like this, you give a moment's space to life so it can organize itself according to your best interests. Don't be surprised if within even moments of reading this, you suddenly notice things swinging your way again.

You are now blessed with the ineffable miracle of your own existence.

instant enlightenment — 4

You are blessed with faith in yourself

That moment of choice between insinuating yourself into the crowd or pulling away to be with yourself, and the underlying question of whether or not you're missing out by doing so – that urge to dive into the midst of the throng not quite managing to beat the urge to withdraw, inevitably accompanied by five to thirty minutes of asking yourself if you've done the right thing or not – do you ever get that?

Fundamentally it's to do with how much faith you have in the choices you make and even more fundamentally with how much faith you have in the idea that wherever you are is wherever you're meant to be, and that you can't miss out on anything because it all goes on inside you anyway.

Say, 'I have the faith' and carry on as you were.

You are now blessed with faith in yourself.

instant enlightenment — 5

You are blessed with the breath of life itself

You set out on a journey aeons ago and have been out on the road for longer than you can remember, but you can remember home and what it feels like – the omnipresent quality of it, the warmth of it, the feeling that everything, at the profoundest level, is OK – the visceral knowing that the world's your oyster.

Stay in touch by maintaining a constant low level of attention on your breathing no matter what else you're up to at the time, moment by moment – this one for a start. Carry on consciously breathing like this and the world is your oyster.

I was going to say trust me on that one – but don't trust me, trust yourself – and you develop that (self-trust), patiently, through the breathing.

You are now blessed with the breath of life itself.

instant enlightenment ——6

You are blessed with beginner's mind

As well as developing self-trust, it's also vital to train yourself increasingly to notice and appreciate what's around you as if you're a small child seeing it all for the first time – practising 'beginner's mind', as they call it in Zen circles.

Decide to let every sight, smell, sound and touch fill you with gleeful awe as if you've never experienced anything like it – because in reality you haven't, however much you think you may have – then trust yourself to have an unprecedented adventure full of the most magnificent surprises, this very day or night, and you will.

You are now blessed with beginner's mind.

instant enlightenment 7

You are blessed with being here

It's easy to say, 'Do less, be more!' but you can't sit staring all day and night when you have things to do.

Always, there is this dance between being and doing – between yin and yang – between the need for freedom and the yearning for structure.

Sanity does not consist in identifying with, or following either urge to its extreme, but in remaining centred at the core of yourself, serenely observing, without prejudice, the swing between the yin and the yang, between the being and the doing.

Breathing freely helps this, as does relaxing the body and, to add extra light to the experience (for that's what each moment is), it helps to determine a positive feeling tone in the mind, achieved by simply stating, 'I choose to feel positive now about being here and doing well what needs to be done, no matter the external circumstances nor the thoughts in my mind.'

You are now blessed with being here.

instant enlightenment 8

You are blessed with intensity of experience

It's really quite remarkable the level of intensity you can generate in the adventure of your life if you really put your mind to it.

So don't hold back. This is the only life you have in your current form. Visualize the most magnificent adventure you can possibly imagine – then start doing things, one small step at a time, to make it come true. What is there to lose? (Other than the dubious security of remaining within your comfort zone.)

You are now blessed with intensity of experience.

instant enlightenment ──9──

You are blessed with expansive

presence

Sit or stand straight now, by lengthening your spine with your mind. Feel the top of your head floating upwards like a helium-filled balloon and your shoulders and hips broadening more with each successive breath you take and release, so that gradually you feel yourself growing exponentially larger. As you continue to breathe – slowly, deeply, silently, flowingly and evenly, without holding your breath for a second – start to see yourself expanding larger than your physical frame and larger still, until you're bigger than the room, the building, street, town, county, province, nation, state, continent, planet, solar system, galaxy and so on, until you fill the entire universe. Then sitting serenely, say, 'I now fill the entire universe and the universe fills me!'

Now retaining awareness of your centre, just below the navel, go about your business, including all your interactions with the people and phenomena you encounter or think about, within the universal largeness of your expansive presence.

You are now blessed with expansive presence.

instant enlightenment —10—

*You are blessed with the
perfection of imperfection*

You become spoilt and entertain unrealistic expectations about the ride – that it should always be smooth, unobstructed and comfortable. But there will always be rough, obstructed, uncomfortable passages and you know that. So why do you insist on deluding yourself to the contrary and then getting all worked up when things get difficult?

Because you're addicted to the chemicals released through dissatisfaction. It's true – why else would you cause yourself so much unnecessary suffering?

So how about this: next time you feel like winding yourself up about how hard and nasty your life is compared to how you think it should be – and watch carefully because it's insidious and creeps up on you without you even noticing – remind yourself that indulging this feeling is just giving yourself a fix that'll leave you weak and shaken. Remind yourself you have a choice. You can instead resist the urge and breathe, in full acceptance of life exactly as it is right now, however imperfect-seeming, and say *thanks* – not to anyone in particular, the Tao doesn't care if you thank it or not, it's not proud and will continue generating existence regardless – but just to be in a thankful state.

Because you never know how long you've got left to enjoy it, you really don't, so waste not another minute feeling anything other than damn perfect (exactly as you are right now) – perfectly imperfect in a perfectly imperfect world.

You are now blessed with the perfection of imperfection.

instant enlightenment 11

You are blessed with all the
information you need to take
your next step on the path

Imagine being aware of every single thing that's going on all the time – not just on this planet but throughout the entire universe – as you tried to make yourself a simple cup of tea.

Well, that's what the Tao, the ineffable presence permeating, informing, animating and connecting all phenomena and non-phenomena, is doing every single day (and night).

Visualize a pair of sliding doors at the crown of your head, slowly opening, and as they do, see yourself downloading from source all the information you need to carry you forth on your path now. Then close your eyes and draw awareness back into the centre of your brain, relax your body, regulate your breathing, ask a question and wait in the silence for the answer, which may come in a flash of images, as a thought, as an entire paragraph spelt out, or simply as a strong feeling in your gut.

You are now blessed with all the information you need to take your next step on the path.

instant enlightenment 12

You are blessed with poke

When you feel stuck, and wish to change the conditions of your life but aren't feeling pokey enough to get started, begin giving yourself the extra poke required by taking a small dab of French mustard on the end of your tongue to lend your system a bit of heat, and repeating 18 times, 'I create my own reality and can create it any way I choose now.' Then, providing you choose to include having enough patience in that, and providing you're willing to show enough fortitude, over time, the conditions of your external reality will gradually shift in a series of surprising quantum leaps, until you find yourself saying, 'Well, blow me down with a feather, just look what I've managed to manifest here!'

You are now blessed with poke.

instant enlightenment 13

You are blessed with the power to change your world

Engaging in violence to achieve change, no matter the ideology it professes to champion, will never achieve anything worthwhile. Engaging in holistic medicine, on the other hand, as just one example of the soft option for making change, can achieve much that's worthwhile.

There will, however, always be violence in the world as long as you or I have violence within us. The outer merely reflects the inner.

So imagine a microcosmic quantum event occurring within you now, causing an unprecedented sea change in your psychic balance, where all of a sudden, all your latent, or active, negative, violent, fearful and life-diminishing impulses recede and disappear – we all have them – to be replaced by positive, healing, compassionate, life-affirming ones instead.

Now imagine a similar macrocosmic quantum event occurring spontaneously in the world on the psychic planes, causing an unprecedented sea change in the atmosphere, and all of a sudden the force of darkness and violence that's been trying to sweep the planet recedes and disappears and all who want to maim and kill are beset by acute amnesia so they totally forget the whole thing and go and retrain in holistic medicine or whatever instead.

Then say, 'As I imagine it, so will it be,' and carry on as you were.

It's just a game but it's fun, and far more energetically and metaphysically healthy for everyone involved than focusing on the violence within you or without, for what you focus on grows.

You are now blessed with the power to change your world.

instant enlightenment — 14

You are blessed with lightness of being

You think that all those thoughts in your forebrain, all that constant internal natter is who you are, which is fine when the conversation's going well, but when it's not – when you find yourself fighting with your own mind – it causes you stress and misery.

You think your body and all its actions and functions is who you are, which is fine momentarily as you gaze in the mirror and all looks well, or you walk down the street with a sway in your hips, but when you're looking or feeling rough, or both, that too causes you stress and misery.

You think your personality, your quips, your gags and *bon mots* are who you are, which is fine when you're on a roll, but when you're feeling shy or out of your element and the ability to engage in social intercourse deserts you, that too causes you stress and misery.

You think your money, your home, your car, your clothes, your artifacts are who you are, which is fine as long as you have them, but when you don't, that too causes you stress and misery.

You think your relationships are who you are, which is fine when harmony rules, but when disharmony rules, that also causes you stress and misery.

Let your 'self', this illusory being composed of all the above, disappear. Become merely a vessel of pure consciousness through which words are spoken or written, healing is administered, actions are performed and, when you remember, love, kindness and pleasure are transmitted and received. It's actually very nice – not having yourself in the way of what you're doing.

You are now blessed with lightness of being.

instant enlightenment

You are blessed with forward

momentum

Onwards and upward, let the journey begin. 'You seem to lead, so … where to?' you ask, following the Tao as gently as you can manage. Begin inside (inwards, onwards and upwards), stilling the mind, relaxing the body, regulating the breathing and allowing the picture of what you want to form itself just in front of the central brain region. When the picture has formed enough to be recognized as a shape, place the shape in a frame of white-gold light and allow it to diminish in size until it is no more than a tiny pinprick of light, which you place and retain in the centre of your forehead. Then say, 'This, or something even better, is now being made manifest', and carry on as you were, being as kind as you can to those around you, and watch the show unfold.

You are now blessed with forward momentum.

instant enlightenment ― 16

You are blessed with the fruits of being fully here in the moment

Relax your body as you read this: let your buttocks go and soften the internal muscles of your pelvic floor, soften your lower back and your belly, take a moment to actually feel your sex-organs – I mean feel with your mind, not your hand (not that would make you blind or cause a war) – and allow your breathing to settle down and become regular and slow. Then, if you can withdraw your awareness back from your eyeballs into the centre of your brain for a minute, you'll notice that all the internal chatter in your forebrain becomes entirely irrelevant. Your experience of being where you are at this very moment originates from a far deeper place instantaneously. Now life has greater depth and your being here feels different, more energized. Your interactions with others will now be authentic and valuable and you'll all get what you want more easily as a result.

You are now blessed with the fruits of being fully here in the moment.

instant enlightenment 17

You are blessed with unshakeable equilibrium

Sometimes things seem to go against you; sometimes they appear to go your way.

'Seem' and 'appear' because this is only the world of the ten thousand things, the world of illusion (even though it still hurts when you bang your head, illusion or not – it's a very clever illusion).

A stance you might like to adopt is the 'not necessarily good, not necessarily bad' approach.

Be in no rush to draw conclusions about good or bad. As things happen, however awful or delightful, observe and remain calm in your centre – enjoy the picture show, but suspend judgement because, as you know, every cloud has a silver lining and every silver lining has a cloud; what looks good at night may look bad in the morning and what looks good in the morning may look bad at night; yin becomes yang and yang becomes yin – it's all relative – not necessarily bad, not necessarily good. Do this and unshakeable equilibrium will be yours for evermore.

You are now blessed with unshakeable equilibrium.

instant enlightenment — 18 —

You are blessed with the very essence of good sense

Picture this: one by one, with exponentially increasing rapidity, people all over the world are waking up to the reality of spirit within and, as they do, the essence of pure consciousness is becoming ever more palpable and, as it does, the levels of conflict both around the globe and within you instantaneously reduce themselves of themselves and everything suddenly takes a remarkable turn for the better.

Like that image?

See enlightenment for everyone, or at least just enough to cause everyone, and I mean absolutely everyone including you and I, to question themselves deeply before attempting to take any course that would harm others, to suddenly stop and say, 'If I hurt another, I am diminishing my own spirit, I am diminishing my own life. If I love my sister or brother, I am causing myself to grow beyond all confines!' or, at least to realize how wasteful and stupid it is to hurt others no matter the reason.

You are now blessed with the very essence of good sense.

instant enlightenment 19

You are blessed with the deep

peace of acquiescence

There's a place you can get to inside when you've taken your foot off the brake for long enough to glide through the traffic of life like a dolphin on wheels, when even though the traffic is heavy and snarled (the pressures of life are intense), you can still find yourself relaxed and rolling with it without resisting too much. This can only happen when you override self-pity and resentment about life not being perfect. And you can only do that when you're willing to trust the benevolence of the road. So even stuck in its traffic, you acknowledge this is where you're meant to be – even inundated by external pressures, you give thanks for simply being here to experience it all.

Breathe in. Look within and around you at your life now. Say thank you.

You are now blessed with the deep peace of acquiescence.

instant enlightenment — 20

You are blessed with limitless abundance

Imagine you are the sea and visualize the rivers flowing towards you, but instead of bringing you loads of dirty, filthy water, they're bringing you loads of high-denomination banknotes of any stable currency of your choice. See yourself as an abundant sea of money and you will be – you'll see, Sea.

But don't stop with money – I only mentioned it first to grab your attention. See the rivers bring you health, love, pleasure, longevity, clarity, joy, and everything else you want too.

Then see how everyone else in the world is equally part of that same sea and see the rivers deliver everything everyone wants for themselves.

You are now blessed with limitless abundance.

instant enlightenment — 21

You are blessed with the power
of inner vision

If you can enter fully into your third eye, the original cavity of spirit in the dead centre of your brain, you can heal everything about yourself. But it's a big if, and one you can only achieve by practice. So saying, make a start even now – pull your awareness back into your centre brain region, relax your chest and sink your energy into your lower belly. This is the ability to return to centre in the midst of events.

Returning to centre is something you can do in a jiffy. Liberating yourself from suffering occurs in the twinkling of an eye. Manifesting things, though, does seem to take quite a while longer. So be patient and calm and everything you wish for, including your being healed or made whole, will manifest without delay and fill you with great glee.

You are now blessed with the power of inner vision.

instant enlightenment 22

You are blessed with the capacity to appreciate even the mundane

If the world as you know it were to come to an end now – if the infrastructure broke down and there were no more shops, transport or commerce – which would be the hundred things you'd miss the most?

Forming this particular list will show you how many things you take for granted and remind you to appreciate more the material benefits and privileges of your existence as it is. It will remind you to value the incredibly elaborate, yet highly vulnerable nature of the life support system you have here.

You are now blessed with the capacity to appreciate even the mundane.

instant enlightenment — 23

You are blessed with the miracle of healing

Feel how you're fighting with yourself and fighting with reality. Feel how it translates into physical tension in your chest, your skull, your face, your throat, your shoulders, your back, your belly, your buttocks, your thighs and even your feet, hands and genitals.

Make a choice now. Say, 'I choose to resolve this conflict now.'

Then simply breathe in, feeling all the physical tension of the fight, and as you breathe out, release it. Release it from your chest, skull, face, throat, shoulders, back, belly, buttocks, thighs, feet, hands, genitals and anywhere else you feel it lingering.

Then, when you've reached a moment of calm, visualize, for the world in general, a drastic reduction in global conflict. Visualize a sudden sea change in the collective mind towards enlightenment and many miracles of healing for everyone, including you – miracles rather than ordinary linear, incremental steps – you live in a miraculous universe, not a mechanical one – and for you, a series of totally unexpected delights in all aspects of your life.

You are now blessed with the miracle of healing.

instant enlightenment —24—

You are blessed with enjoying the weather, whatever

Wilhelm Reich, protégée of Freud, developed a practice of freeing up *chi* (energy) from wherever it has been stuck in the patient's body so it 'streams' freely, thus removing any neurosis and enabling a full orgasm, the ability to attain which, Reich believed to be a benchmark of overall health. That old Wilhelm Reich was so advanced in his experiments with *chi* that he developed a mechanism called an orgone box, which, when aimed at the clouds, was actually able, through the *chi* transmitted, to disperse them – or so it's said.

If however you haven't developed such power over your *chi* yet, or have but would feel presumptuous using it, simply relax and enjoy the weather, literally and metaphorically, exactly as it is, come rain, come shine. You and you only are responsible for your moment-to-moment experience of life, which goes on within you and not outside of you, partly in response to, partly in spite of, external conditions, come what may.

'I am in command of my own experience of life.'

Say it a few times and feel the power of realization course through your veins.

You are now blessed with enjoying the weather, whatever.

You are blessed with centredness in the midst of events

Would it be boring here if we didn't have all these lunatics playing around with guns and bombs? Would the story lose all dynamic tension if it weren't for the ever-present threat of annihilation?

Why can't we leave each other, or ourselves, in peace? Why do people get so hungry for status, power and wealth they'll stop at nothing to get it? Can it be just to give the group story-line more bite? It must just be our nature, for nature, in all its guises, is as demonically destructive as it's angelically construc-tive and, indeed, has to be for things not to overgrow their space and run amok.

The key, in the midst of the universal dance of equilibrium between destruction and construction, is to keep breathing deeply, fluently, evenly and smoothly, never holding the breath unless under water or during a chemical attack, and allowing that to keep you constantly connected to your tao within. This will create the perfect milieu for you to remain centred in the midst of events.

You are now blessed with centredness in the midst of events.

instant enlightenment 26

You are blessed with swift progress in all your endeavours

No matter what you want – peace, health, wealth, accomplishment, beauty, pleasure, love, possessions, popularity, whatever – it all begins within. And it's not selfish to create it. If just one person can reach a state of being utterly at peace with themselves, the whole world can – so meditate.

Be mindful of returning to the silence in the very depths of your mind, beneath the clatter and clamour of the everyday inner dialogue, during the cracks in your busy day and night. Spend brief moments breathing with an empty mind – it could just be one breath in and one out after a phone call, text message or email – during which you relax into the majesty of being, before making the next phone call. Gradually, perhaps over a few lifetimes and many, many phone calls, that inner silence becomes the norm and then peace will reign.

All true change happens slowly from the perspective of linear time, but from the perspective of eternity, one glimpses a series of quantum leaps.

You are now blessed with swift progress in all your endeavours.

instant enlightenment 27

You are blessed with living in remarkable times

No matter all the micro-crises affecting you, the real crisis going on behind the scenes is the worldwide ecological disaster waiting to happen, as global warming increases exponentially and pollution kills off all known life except for rats and spiders. Not that I want to alarm you – just to point out the absurdity of what you tend to focus on in light of the enormity of the real issues.

The key to sanity, to retrieving a sane perspective during such times, is obviously not to freak yourself out being scared of things that may never happen – after all, we may find a way out of our predicament – but to centre yourself with body awareness and conscious breathing and remind yourself to appreciate the air you breathe, the water you drink, the food you eat, the electricity and oil you burn, knowing that it could all be gone in the blink of an eye, anytime now. Do this and your time here, each and every moment of it, will be remarkable.

You are now blessed with living in remarkable times.

instant enlightenment 28

You are blessed with agility

In this world of the ten thousand things, the world of changing forms – for all forms do change over time – how extraordinary it is to put your heart and soul into things, while being aware that conditions could change so rapidly you could be living in a cave or dustbin before the day's out. Not that it's likely that will happen, but you never know on a planet like this. You have to stay agile, flexible and unattached to goals and the way you think things should be – this, at the deepest level of your being – if you wish to remain balanced on the tightrope of life.

You do what you do because you have to do something or you grow quickly restless. You play the game of having and reaching goals for all you're worth, otherwise what's the point of playing it – and in any case you'd probably starve if you didn't – but you always remember it's just a game, because that gives you the lightness of mind to be agile.

You are now blessed with agility.

instant enlightenment — 29

You are blessed with renewal

This world is but a dream. You know it but forget it from time to time, so wrapped up do you get in the addictive nature of material reality. While this may not seem such a big deal to you, the Buddhists, Taoists and Hindus have always laid great store by it, calling this realm, respectively, the world of illusion, the world of the ten thousand things, and samsara.

They place great emphasis on remembering it's all only relative here on the earth plane where all forms change over time. The only thing that's actually real and unchanging is the underlying meta-conscious, generative force behind the earth plane dream, but if you simply allow yourself a moment's respite here and now with that sole thought held firmly in the centre of your brain ('this is all but a dream') you will be instantaneously restored and able to re-enter the affray with clarity renewed and vigour and vim refreshed.

You are now blessed with renewal.

instant enlightenment 30

You are blessed with integrity

Every moment – this one for instance – you are at a crossroads faced with a choice. Do you listen to your instincts and intuition and follow what they tell you, come what may, or do you go with the crowd regardless?

Every moment, you are faced with potential ruin on account of sticking to what your instincts and intuition tell you. Choose to feel empowered rather than weakened by this – don't let it perturb you unduly, unless you enjoy the sensation of perturbation. You've been here before many times. Sometimes you've even caved in, thinking the crowd must be right, even though it didn't feel that way – and regretted it later. What you probably learned from the ensuing discomfort, was that it's better to be out on your ear in the street with your integrity intact than ensconced in a palace with it in tatters.

Because when your integrity with your tao or path is sound, the adventure will develop and lead you swiftly to fresh and better pastures.

You are now blessed with integrity.

You are blessed with the power
to overcome any obstacle

If you want it, you now have easy access to your innate confidence, to clear awareness of what you know to be right for you, and to the strength to stay with the process of materializing it, even in the face of any obstacle. That you may not be feeling that way right now and probably aren't, is just the result of negative thoughts affecting your perspective and energy levels.

Visualize three treasure chambers, one in the centre of your chest, one in the depths of your belly and one in the centre of your brain. Open the door to the chamber in your chest and you access the very essence of confidence. Open the door to the chamber in your belly and you access the very essence of strength. Open the door to the chamber in your brain and you access the very essence of awareness.

These are *a priori*, universal qualities, present throughout existence, which, simply using your imagination, you now access at will through your body.

You are now blessed with the power to overcome any obstacle.

instant enlightenment — 32

You are blessed with a cheerful heart

You have an incredible facility for continuing with your life as normal during such abnormal times as these, when nothing is certain but change. But normal and abnormal are only relative terms. In reality, there are no normal times. Normality is just an illusion you cling to to help you try and make sense of it all and keep things as neat, tidy and manageable as you can. The illusion of normality is merely a theatrical device – a construct in other words, and a damn fine one too. But what if you abandon it momentarily and accept instead that nothing is normal and anything could happen – and probably will? Then, rather than lament that and fight against it, what would happen if you accepted and even welcomed it?

Ah, then, the zen!

In this milieu of the unexpected, go forth as a warrior this very minute with a cheerful heart and an optimistic frame of mind.

You are now blessed with a cheerful heart.

instant enlightenment 33

*You are blessed with loving
whatever's happening*

Your self-doubt is merely an addiction to the set of internal chemicals released during any good self-doubting session.

If you find you're not enjoying the buzz anymore, the first step is to relax your body, slow down your breath and acknowledge that it's self-doubt you're trying to get high on. The next step is to allow yourself to enjoy the physical feeling. Then the self-doubt evaporates as enjoyment takes over and here you are again, simply breathing and being here.

Practising such techniques for in-the-moment enlightenment doesn't prevent life sneaking up from behind and banging you on the head occasionally when it feels like it, but it does help you recover and regain your equilibrium far quicker. The key is to love it. This requires easing off for a moment and returning awareness to the breath. Breathing in and out evenly, silently, smoothly and graciously, each and every moment.

So as both global and personal dramas unfold around and within you, you simply keep breathing and remain centred. Easy to say – easy to do. It's all just down to remembering.

This was to remind you.

You are now blessed with loving whatever's happening.

instant enlightenment 34

You are blessed with immunity

To build your immune system, the main contributory factors involved are:

One: regular daily holistic exercise, including working out intelligently, chi gung, running, tai chi, yoga, swimming, walking and anything else that engages body, mind and breath simultaneously

Two: relaxing (as opposed to collapsing) while on the run – making sure, in other words, that you don't use up unnecessary energy

Three: restricting all internal dialogue to pleasant conversation – no beating yourself up

Four: eating food with the energy still in it – fresh fruit, vegetables, sprouts, organic meat – and avoiding eating too much lifeless crap

Five: turning the shower to extreme cold for a few moments during morning ablutions and breathing out fiercely like a woman in labour until your body temperature rises enough to burn off the bugs

Six: focusing your intention on staying alive and healthy by regular repetition of such sentiments as, 'I choose health!' and by visualizing yourself surviving, even thriving throughout. However, don't succumb to fear about your own mortality. Develop trust in the wisdom of your particular destiny and grace to accept that when it's your time to leave, it's your time to leave.

You are now blessed with immunity.

instant enlightenment 35

You are blessed with limitless wealth

Picture yourself sitting peacefully, receptively and expectantly against the expansive trunk of a fat old oak in summertime, its branches forming a vast canopy above you. The sky is blue, the sun is shining and you feel warm and safe.

Look up at the leaves on the branches, copious in amount, but strange in appearance. 'What is it?' you ask. As you focus, you realize each leaf is actually a shiny new high-denomination banknote of any stable currency of your choice. Then the most remarkable thing happens. As you sit there, these notes start falling from the tree, forming large piles around you. As one note falls a fresh one instantaneously replaces it. What a miraculous tree this is! Stuff your pockets gracefully and grate-fully, get up from the ground and carry on as you were, know-ing you can return to collect more any time you choose.

The effects of this visualization tend to occur within three weeks – money flow in your direction simply increases, often in contradiction of logic, and you find that somehow the books balance themselves out.

The subtext of this, of course, is that material reality is an elastic affair. It responds to the inner realm and what you do in there. Make the inner rich and expansive, abundant and full of fine fruit and the outer will respond accordingly. The delay is simply because in the inner realm energy/thought moves freely, while in the outer realm, energy/thought has to be processed through loads of matter and other people's agendas before it manifests for you. Being generous to those around you helps speed up the process.

You are now blessed with limitless wealth.

instant enlightenment 36

*You are blessed immediately
with a magnificent surprise*

Something wonderful is about to happen – a magnificent surprise is coming your way – something you weren't counting on – something to light up the whole of your life and fill your heart with love and joy. So take a deep breath, then breathe out.

Then repeat that and keep repeating it till you die. Let the unexpected occur.

Wonderful things are happening all the time – your very existence to name but one – something you may take for granted but which is without doubt, when you consider the heavy odds against it in such a ferocious universe as this, the most magnificently surprising event possible. Think about it: consciousness, etc., a body in and with which to enjoy it and a life-supporting planet of indescribable beauty and variation to enjoy it on. From this perspective, it instantly becomes clear how every hitherto trivial-seeming event in your day-to-day and night-to-night existence, is in fact a magnificent surprise.

Focus on the magnificently surprising nature of all the myriad details of your existence now and it will grow.

You are now blessed immediately with a magnificent surprise.

instant enlightenment — 37

You are blessed with protection

from the madness of the world

What is this urge to draw each other in? It's natural, that's obvious. If we didn't have a natural person-drawing instinct we'd never be able to organize ourselves as a society. Ideas, which, after all, originate in one person's mind, would never find enough agreement with others to be enacted. Or maybe it's the basic organizing instinct that comes first and the propensity to draw others in follows as an effect.

It doesn't matter.

What does, in the light of all the crazy bastards running round the planet, is to be able to avoid being drawn in to the madness that happens around you and to do your best to maintain an easy, effortless, non-invasive and generally loving vibe in your immediate environment, and trust it to be infectious.

In the game of drawing in, you either draw or get drawn. Let your place be to stand firm and draw others into your positive force field.

You are now blessed with protection from the madness of the world.

instant enlightenment 38

You are blessed with the

freshness of pastures new

If you've been daring enough to take command of your own life and set off on your own adventure, you'll find yourself having to let go of much of the old in your life as the new pushes its way into the picture. Most of the time it feels beautiful, but some of the time it feels damn weird.

But sod it; damn weird's a small price to pay for magic. You're in the throws or meta-transformation, a pleasant passage into fresh pastures and a gracious, easy letting go of whatever and whoever needs to be released from your orbit, right now, to enable you to move on.

What a poignantly tasty dish of sweet and sour chicken this life can be – with compassion as your pair of chopsticks – compassion for yourself as well as others. In fact if you don't have compassion for yourself, you can't really have it for others either.

Be deeply daring now.

You are now blessed with the freshness of pastures new.

You are blessed with staying alive and in the game, come what may

Seize on the idea of staying alive and in the game, no matter what, as being the fundamental goal, if indeed, there is one, of your physical reality. Start to motivate yourself by affirming, 'I choose to stay alive and in the game, come what may!'

Repeat it a few times till you mean it and you'll notice that you've started to enjoy the sensation of insecurity that comes with being alive – it's become exciting.

Stop holding your breath now and surrender into the loving arms of the Tao, the Great Mother of existence and non-existence, and everything will be OK.

You are now blessed with staying alive and in the game, come what may.

instant enlightenment 40

You are blessed with

instantaneous manifestation

Acceleration is in the air, not so much in terms of wind as in terms of the action speeding up, and you can already feel it in your belly – not in terms of wind, but in terms of responding to the accelerating energy in the air, accelerating as smoothly and calmly as practiced lovers approaching mutual orgasm.

If you feel you don't already have one, spend a moment choosing a direction towards which you feel like moving in your life from here, so that you may take full advantage of the acceleration in affairs this time in history offers.

Then slow down almost to a standstill inside. Start with the breathing and let it decelerate to half time and let the swirl of thoughts in your forebrain follow. The slower you can be inside, the faster the outside will move, until it's moving so fast, what you want materializes almost faster than you can wish for it.

You are now blessed with instantaneous manifestation.

instant enlightenment 41

You are blessed with the golden touch

Always the subtext – will you win or will you lose?

If that rings a bell for you, perhaps you'd care to join me in repeating the following affirmation, one of my favourites, one which generally works a treat at times you think you're losing:

'I am always in the right place at the right time, successfully engaged in the right activity with the right result for me and everyone.'

And if you say it a few times with feeling, you'll probably notice yourself calming down and settling into the moment. However, if that doesn't do the trick, try:

'I choose to feel peace in my heart and my soul – I choose to feel peace in my heart and my soul – I choose to feel peace in my heart and my soul – I choose to feel calm in my body, yeah, yeah – I choose to feel calm in my body'.

Then all you have to do is breathe more deeply and freely, relax your body and carry on with your day and night – and everything you touch will turn to gold.

You are now blessed with the golden touch.

instant enlightenment 42

You are blessed with total immersion

If you watch carefully now, you'll see the very atoms shimmering in the air around you. If you see it, what you're looking at are impressions made by the rustling of the skirts of the Great Mother of all existence and non-existence, as she wafts by you.

You can talk to her if you like – she won't mind a bit – and if you're really quiet, you'll hear her talking back to you, telling you everything's alright, it really is. And no matter the darkness in your mind, no matter the fearful thoughts you may be entertaining, no matter, even, the pain in your heart or your body, you will be soothed.

Breathe now – stop holding your breath – let it flow evenly, silently, deeply, let it be utterly smooth and silent. Now, using a spare thought, concentrate lightly on the idea of expelling pain with every out breath and inhaling strength, health, peace, love and plenty as you breathe in.

Eventually, say, 'Yes, Barefoot Doctor, this is going to be a damn good day or night – in fact, it already is!'

So don't hang about – immerse yourself in it – surrender to its pull, enjoy it and give thanks.

You are now blessed with total immersion.

instant enlightenment —43—

You are blessed with an inner landscape of great splendour

It's a mystery – how you got here, where you came from, where you're going, why you're going there, why you were born into the life you were born into and whether there is such a thing as destiny … or whether it's all just one huge chain reaction, a pattern of cause and effect that began the very moment the universe sprang into existence, that has eventually led inevitably to where you are now … or simply just a random accident. And no matter how many clever people try to solve it, it will always remain unsolvable. That's the game, the Rubik cube of existence. But don't let that be your focus today or tonight, unless you're enjoying the physical sensation that thinking about it generates within you.

Otherwise, simply do things one at a time in as much of a rational sequence as you can muster, starting with choosing a day and night of inner splendour, no matter what occurs around you.

You are now blessed with an inner landscape of great splendour.

instant enlightenment —44—

You are blessed with inner warmth

Do you ever give yourself acknowledgement? I don't mean silently, in your imagination, but out loud? It's given wisdom that talking aloud to yourself is the first sign of insanity. However, it's not the talking that indicates insanity, it's what you say and the way you say it. Sure, it's insane to be nasty to yourself, but being kind and loving – could that be insane?

Have a go at your earliest opportunity. Big yourself up a bit this very day or night. Tell yourself out loud what a totally wonderful person you are. Congratulate yourself for being here, for withstanding the awesome forces lined up against you – the solar winds, the asteroids, the earthquakes, the pollution, the stress, the inland revenue, the suicide bombers – and say, 'Well done, you!'

You are now blessed with inner warmth.

instant enlightenment 45

You are blessed with backbone

No matter how you spend your time, the intention to contribute something of value is paramount. Are you important in the eyes of the world? It's patently clear that as long as you give out the love, you're important. Nothing else really counts.

In any case, the last thing you want to carry around as you trundle along the Great Thoroughfare of Life is the burden of self-importance.

Everything you experience along the way is actually, in essence, nothing more than a trick of the light, a vast sleight of hand by the supreme conjuror for your amusement and bemusement. Let any nervousness about this within be well matched by strength in your backbone – say, 'Backbone, be strong!' immediately, and feel it to be so and you will manifest everything you want easily, effortlessly and charmingly.

You are now blessed with backbone.

instant enlightenment 46

You are blessed with freedom
from constriction

If you're feeling somehow constricted in your life at present, remind yourself that the nature of life on earth for humans, as well as for everyone else around here, is cyclical and under the direct command of the immutable law of yin and yang. Yin represents the force of contraction innate in all phenomena and situations; yang represents expansion. Just like night and day, neither can go on forever without eventually turning into its opposite. Hence the value of reminding yourself by way of affirmation – out of contraction comes expansion.

So choose an expansive day and night now. Feel as expansive as the endless space that surrounds you as you hurtle through the universe this very second, on a planet that's moving at 66,000 miles per hour while spinning on its axis at 1,000 miles per hour. Feel as expansive as all the endless opportunities that lie in wait for you just around the corner.

You are now blessed with freedom from constriction.

instant enlightenment 47

You are blessed with transformation

A shift of consciousness and energy, originating at the deepest level of the Tao, is about to be enacted on the human stage. You can't yet know what will happen as a result of it, but if you become silent enough inside you can hear its power within you. Have a moment of tuning in, in order to align yourself more effectively so you can take full advantage of it when it manifests.

Lengthen your spine, relax all your muscles, slow down your breathing, look into the space between and behind your eyes and with a warm, open heart see a picture of approximately 6.2 billion children of all ages from zero to 135, including you and I, all doing the very best they can do, each according to her or his current stage of personal evolution and circumstances, stumbling along in the dark, holding each others' hands for mutual comfort and support. Then from your warm, open heart, send them all, including you and I, a wave of compassion and love – (thank you).

As you re-enter normal waking state, imagine you've come to on a different planet altogether. Everything looks the same, smells the same, sounds the same, handles the same to the touch, yet it all feels distinctly, subtly different from the place you're used to. It's as if someone switched planets on you while you were contemplating. As you go about your business from here, you notice a definite change for the better in the way people are interacting with each other – you notice a deeper quality of consciousness in the group mind and an atmosphere of mutual respect.

You are now blessed with transformation.

instant enlightenment — 48

You are blessed with a
command of life's details

If you could gather up all the details of your existence – all the tax stuff, the forms, the official crap, the money, the passports, credit cards and driving licenses, the insurance policies, the personal issues, the agreements, the disagreements, the grudges, the gripes, the clothes, the shoes, the socks, the cosmetics – and everything else you can think of – and put them all in one place, and if everyone else on the planet was able to and did so too, how vast would the pile be? Eight universes' worth? Twenty-three?

Yes, imagine life without all the details you and everyone else endlessly chase. The ancient Taoists called this realm of details the world of the ten thousand things. They taught that instead of focusing your energy there, you should focus it on the stillness at the centre of your being and all the details will take care of themselves. (That's the basic idea. In reality, you'll probably find you still have to write endless lists.)

You are now blessed with a command of life's details.

instant enlightenment 49

You are blessed with all the time you need

As a small child, did you ever have a go at one of those strange old games at the end of the pier in the amusement arcade, with the glass cage and mechanical hand, where you had 50 seconds or so to try and grab one of the prizes lying on the bottom, and did you invariably come away empty-handed with that awful sinking feeling of time running out before you had a chance to get what you wanted?

Did you ever hear the line, 'A hundred summers when they're done will seem as short as a single one'?

Have you been aware of the sensation of time moving extremely quickly of late and realized you've been racing internally to get everything done, as if the game is about to end at any time? How silly. Instead, become aware of the relativity of time and space and the preciousness of simply being, whatever results that may, or may not, produce.

This is a good moment to still the mind, to draw your awareness backwards into the central region of the brain, allowing the forebrain to rest from all its habitual internal chatter. Still carry on with what you have to do, but no longer expend energy on involving yourself in the noise and clamour that normally occupies your mind – simply watch in stillness. To support such an internal stance, it helps enormously to slow down and regulate the breathing tempo and relax all your muscles. No longer caught up in the illusion of racing, you are thus centred.

You are now blessed with all the time you need.

instant enlightenment 50

You are blessed with a dose of everything-is-possible

This day (and night) has an air of everything-is-possible about it and requires nothing more than your acceptance of the concept of limitless potential for it to deliver the most unexpected opportunities – a simple opening of the self, a relaxing of the muscular armouring normally used unconsciously to block out the pain – but which also blocks out the pleasure – and a basic willingness to receive in humility the blessing being offered you. Breathing slowly and evenly, you gently welcome the theatre of the day or night and without getting in the way in any way, allow yourself to receive it, come what may.

Transform that into an affirmation to set your mind straight on the mode you're choosing to adopt, in the following way. Say: 'This day has an air of everything-is-possible about it and requires nothing more than my acceptance of limitless potential for it to deliver the most unexpected opportunities – I open myself, relax my muscular armouring and am willing to receive the blessing being offered. I breathe slowly and evenly and gently welcome the theatre now, without getting in the way in any way and allow myself to receive it, come what may.'

You are now blessed with a dose of everything-is-possible.

instant enlightenment 51

You are blessed with
contentment

What does it take to make you stop long enough to feel content to simply be here, even just for a moment, every now and then? How much of your list of 'things to be achieved' has to be crossed off before you can allow yourself the space to be satiated simply by breathing? Achieving things – the attainment of goals – only has a short-term effect on your level of contentment, for as soon as one thing's done there are twenty more waiting to be done, and as soon as you get something it's no longer good enough and you want more.

The only antidote to this restlessness of the soul is to still the mind by relaxing the body, slowing the breath and allowing the thoughts to drift undisturbed and unexamined in the forebrain, while you relocate your awareness in the central region of your brain. Obviously it helps enormously if before doing so you set your intention clearly – in this instance, to release yourself from the pull of the world of appearances, where discontent is the currency, in order to sit in the realm of the unchanging Tao, where contentment and peace reign. Then, when you decide to return yourself to the active state, set your intention to carry that peace through with you so it permeates your mind and actions as you carry on with your business.

I'm telling you this to remind you.

You are now blessed with contentment.

instant enlightenment 52

You are blessed with fulfilment

Instead of habitually and vainly seeking lasting fulfilment in relationships with others, work, possessions, status and all other considerations of the shifting sands of the material world, seek (and find) it anytime in the silence at your core, where the Tao is waiting for you. But for it to mean anything at all, it has to be shared. That's why you have the facility to love – love, as in softening the muscular armour protecting your chest and allowing your warmth not only to radiate to others, but to inform your urges and actions till you find yourself compulsively committing random acts of giving.

It could be a smile, a helping hand, or asking someone what's troubling them and giving them a spontaneous head, neck and shoulder massage – preferably without messing up their hairdo. You're straddling two worlds right now – one foot in the world of the ten thousand things, the other in the impenetrable silence of the Tao. To prevent the two diverging, and causing you to do the splits so much it tears your loins apart – because I'm sure you're rather fond of them – commit a random act of giving now.

You are now blessed with fulfilment.

instant enlightenment —53—

You are blessed with the power
to communicate

You've got to talk about something – at least until you uncover the subtext to your thoughts, to what you perceive to be really going on around here. Which at the deepest level, as far as I can see, is the Tao being the Tao, doing what the Tao does in all its discreet, universal, omnipresent majesty. It's the divine spirit moving within and among us all – and it's the realization of your own divine nature that gives you the motivation and energy to keep going against all the odds like you do.

That's why people get intoxicated and party with each other – so they can more freely converse with each other through words, gestures, music, dance and, of course, sex and by that conversation reach moments of such realization. So my talking to you is a bridge – a bridge between the superficial, local level, where we all appear to be separate individuals and the deeper, universal level, where we are the one being, the Tao, each of us a different aspect or prism of it, each with a different face, set of fingerprints and local life story.

The key to walking across the bridge and getting to the other side where we all meet, is not words, but love. In fact, I'd say that being willing to look beneath the surface to the subtext below, in which we are all merely different expressions of the same Tao, combined with an intention to transmit and receive love, is quite possibly the very best thing you can do on a day (and night) like this.

You are now blessed with the power to communicate.

instant enlightenment 54

You are blessed with something amazing happening

The possibility of water on Mars may not blow your hair back as a concept, but it means that before too long, it's not without the realms of possibility that you'll be able to go and live there – or if not there, at least on the Moon. And while it may not have immediate appeal, consider the pristine conditions, the space, and the lack of pollution. Think of the opportunities.

But then think of all the things you'd miss. The people, the views, even the madness. It makes you appreciate life on this planet, thinking about moving to Mars. It pushes you into a micro-moment of appreciative stillness. In that micro-moment, imagine a breathing aperture in the centre of your chest. Imagine yourself breathing in and out purposefully through it. As you breathe in, imagine you are sucking in the generic quality of universal love into the heart of your very being. As you breathe out, imagine you're emanating that love, multiplied by 108.

Now – not that I'd presume to tell you what to do, but anyway – gird your loins, go out into the garden and be a kind and loving brother or sister to your brothers and sisters who play there with you, so that peace, prosperity, health, wisdom and love among all the peoples of the Earth may prevail!

You are now blessed with something amazing happening.

You are blessed with the discreet exhilaration of following orderly procedures

You have adopted over the years a series of procedures by which you let yourself know you're you – behavioural modules, easily interchanged, to cover the way you go about doing what you have to do in a day and night. The way, for example, you proceed with exercise, sitting down at the computer, standing up again, eating, washing, meeting or greeting and how you move modules around to fit what's happening that day and night, and how the modules form patterns – themselves highly flexible – which stretch over the course of a week, month, year or decade.

There is nothing extraordinary in this – in fact, these procedures are the very pattern of the ordinary.

But at the point of dying, there may be a moment, had you never stopped to appreciate your procedures, when you'd think sadly, 'Damn, I never honoured all those remarkable little procedures of mine, that let me know who I was, and now it's too late!' So love your own procedures more, thereby loving yourself more, and hold on to an awareness of the divine presence of the Tao itself in every procedural step – because love is the key to everything.

You are now blessed with the discreet exhilaration of following orderly procedures.

instant enlightenment 56

You are blessed with whatever you want

Visualize very clearly what it is you want to manifest now – anything you visualize during this time with sufficient gusto will come to pass with startling results.

Pass it on – and if you do tell people, tell them it helps if once you've pictured what you want for yourself, you then picture what you want for the whole world, which hopefully will include peace, love, tolerance, wisdom and abundance prevailing once more.

You are now blessed with whatever you want.

instant enlightenment 57

You are blessed with beauty

You are extremely beautiful, no matter your opinions about the externals. The spirit within you, to whom I'm talking now, is, in fact, nothing but pure beauty.

You may find it a warming experience right now to repeat silently about 108 times, or until you truly feel it reverberate in your very bones, 'I am beautiful', then visualize the primordial essence of the universal quality of beauty enter you through the crown of your head and fill you from head to toe. Visualize it transform your features even as we speak now, informing them with the light of the world and making you so beautiful you actually want to eat yourself.

Don't go changing now …

You are now blessed with beauty.

instant enlightenment —58

You are blessed with being able
to stop

Stop racing for a minute and let your mind slow down.

Do you ever do that?

The key is the breathing – feel it slowing down right now, feel it become soft and smooth like a string of fine round precious pearls moving gently in and out, causing your belly to swell and contract. Then bring your mind into it. Imagine harshness leaving you on the exhalation and softness filling you on the inhalation. Harshness out – softness in.

Next, make an affirmation: 'In stillness, everything comes to pass.' Try saying it silently to yourself, it's nice.

There, for the length of time that took, 30 seconds or so, I was moving much more slowly. How was it for you?

You are now blessed with being able to stop.

instant enlightenment 59

You are blessed with being a real swinger

Withdraw your awareness now into the centre of your brain, into the Cave of the Original Spirit.

All you see when you gaze out from here, in your forebrain and beyond, is the world of the ten thousand things, the world of the mind. See the interplay between the unchanging Tao within the cave – the stillness at the core – and the world of the mind caught in the external world, and notice your addiction to the latter and the internal drugs it releases.

When you allow yourself to get attached to the thoughts swirling in your forebrain, it generates excitement or anxiety, depending on the thoughts and the energetic state of your body. This can be highly seductive and addictive, but if indulged in without a break, will eventually weaken you in mind, body and spirit.

When, on the other hand, you draw your awareness back into the centre of your brain, detach from the swirl of thoughts in the forebrain, soften your breathing and let your energy settle in your belly, if only for 30 seconds or so, you refresh, rejuvenate and restore yourself in mind, body and spirit.

The inevitable swing between these two states can be enjoyed throughout the day and night – this one for instance, and will afford you a much more pleasurable time of it than were you to remain locked in your mind permanently.

Remember, it don't mean a thing if it ain't got that swing.

You are now blessed with being a real swinger.

instant enlightenment 60

You are blessed with evolution

There are only two ways to go from here – regress or evolve. There is no neutral direction. Choose one now. Go with evolution, and you'll notice how evolution is happening within you already on an inner level. Even externally, it's visible in the huge numbers of people exploring their potential through yoga, tai chi, meditation and all the rest of it.

Evolution is painful at first because you have to relinquish the old, much of which was pleasant, comforting and familiar, even if tight fitting. To avoid this pain, it is only natural that some react with fear and hatred and regress with a vengeance – hence the trends towards neo-fundamentalism and neo-fascism.

Soften the effect of this now by sending out compassion for all those who have thus temporarily lost their way. Focus an imaginary beam of brilliant white light and direct it at all the people who have been beguiled into believing in reactionary nonsense, and visualize it purifying all negativity and replacing it with peace and wisdom.

See everyone who is caught in a reactionary syndrome suddenly overcome with love. Love is the only antidote to fear and hatred. For as you see it, if you see it clearly enough, so it will be.

You are now blessed with evolution.

instant enlightenment 61

You are blessed with the grace
of a bumbling fool

In aspiring to living your life as a warrior, it is vital for your health and peace of mind not to berate yourself if you slip up from time to time – just notice, laugh and carry on. This will be enough to disperse, over time, most of the patterns which have hitherto enabled the secret self-saboteur within to scupper your attempts at being graceful and effective in all your actions, words and deeds. Most, but not all. For it amuses the Tao to have you flawed somehow – note flawed, not floored – for without some distortions, what a bland place this would be. Without moments of being bumbling fools, where would come the pleasure from those rare moments of achieving perfection, that so entrance you and me?

Give yourself an easy time of it now.

You are now blessed with the grace of a bumbling fool.

instant enlightenment — 62

You are blessed with deep
enjoyment

You waste tons of energy and time worrying about things that never happen, when you could be using that time and energy to enjoy yourself instead.

And I don't mean hedonistically necessarily (though that can always be fun) – but enjoying yourself at the very deepest level – your soul simply enjoying the opportunity to experience the miracle of being alive in a human body, with a human personality, on an utterly mysterious planet rotating most adroitly, for now, at least, on it's own axis at 1,000 mph, while orbiting the sun (at this very moment) at no less than a staggering 66,000 mph (19 mps).

So just for the next 38 miles or so, stop, breathe, relax, let go, allow. Say, 'Why, thank you! What a damn fine show!' and let drop the blessing of deeply enjoying just being here.

You are now blessed with deep enjoyment.

instant enlightenment 63

You are blessed with the grace of taking one small step at a time

You're getting caught up in the importance of your own life story and it's starting to make you feel uncomfortable. You stop and look – and you realize you have been overriding generous impulses towards others of late – you have been denying them, and you, the mutual flow between you. You think it would be nice to change but haven't the time right now.

But then you think, *Birmingham wasn't built in a day*. You don't have to become enlightened all at once – take it one small step at a time, one gesture of gingerly reaching out after another, until it starts becoming natural for you, and everything will be alright.

Press firmly with your thumb into the dead centre of the opposite palm for 40 seconds on each hand to open up the energy in your heart centre now. Then, thinking of the whole world, let the natural warmth flow from your chest through the palms of your hands. Love – that's what we all want and our mission (if we have one) is to spread that love. Love is all that really matters.

You are now blessed with the grace of taking one small step at a time.

instant enlightenment 64

You are blessed with constant entertainment

'Ah, the brain – what a wonderful thing!' you may occasionally find yourself thinking. After all, without your brain that would have been unlikely. Think about it. See? Isn't it fantastic? That mass of rubbery gloop you could fit in a cereal bowl is what makes this whole experience an experience.

But how often do you ever tell your brain how much you love it? How often do you let it know you care? Probably never. Don't feel guilty though, as negative thoughts just compound the insult by making your brain miserable and tired. Just say, 'Brain, I love you so much,' and then if you go very still, you'll feel your brain respond by lighting up from within and that will make you feel very happy.

However, when you say it, be sure to feel that love anchored deep inside your chest, otherwise the energy in your brain as it swells will overwhelm you. And be sure to anchor the love in your chest to the life force in your belly, otherwise the entire procedure will lack gravitas and your mind will float off into fantasy land.

Then your brain will feel so chipper from being properly acknowledged and so much more loving for being loved, it will entertain you masterfully and with aplomb the whole day and night long.

You are now blessed with constant entertainment.

instant enlightenment 65

*You are blessed with a
beautiful time of it*

Entertain a loving thought about someone and they feel it instantaneously as a subtle wave of happiness and wellbeing. They won't know whence it came or why, but that doesn't matter, only the sending it matters for not only does it increase the flow of happiness and wellbeing back your way, it increases the flow of happiness and wellbeing in the general atmosphere for everyone to enjoy (including you), so you win both ways.

Generally though, if left to its own devices, the mind defaults to the negative mode, forgets about love and becomes critical instead, thus increasing the flow of malaise and stress both your way and in general. The mind needs constant retraining in this respect. Start now.

Think of anyone you know and love now, and as you inhale feel the life force in your body collect as love in your chest, then exhale and feel that love extend from your chest to envelop your vision of the person, till you see them glowing with it, while reminding yourself that by sending love to others, you attract love towards you threefold. That's why I'm suggesting it now, so you have a beautiful time of it.

You are now blessed with a beautiful time of it.

You are blessed with the capacity to handle all the pain of life

All things must come and all things must pass. Forms come together and fall apart. People come together and separate. Clinging causes pain. Releasing engenders grace.

It's a physical thing – you release the tautness in your muscular holding pattern, breathe, let things be, remain in the moment, then grace descends and the pain passes, no matter how great.

It still sucks though. But then they never said life would be a bowl of roses.

On the other hand, it's a hell of a good adventure when you let go and flow with it, even if it does get a bit painful from time to time. Choose this now in spite of all the moments of joy inevitably, eventually, turning into moments of sadness and grief – a rip-roaring adventure of such scale and magnitude you hardly know what to do with yourself in all the excitement, and find yourself handling the pain of separation with equipoise and aplomb.

You are now blessed with the capacity to handle all the pain of life.

instant enlightenment 67

*You are blessed with deep
tranquillity*

See a wide parabolic arc, curving away from you – a wide angle sweep of energy – energy infused with love, love infused with energy, spreading to everyone within its curve, from San Francisco, the long way round to Shanghai, and everywhere in between. Then turn around and let it radiate to the people of the southern hemisphere, from Patagonia to Perth (or Freemantle) as well.

As it spreads across the face of the earth, see it bring soothing and calm to everyone in its path, until every living being is momentarily in a state of deep tranquillity.

Do it as humble servant – someone honoured to be custodian of the divine tranquillizer. As you do, attune yourself to the calm and soothing voice within and hear the words going around and around, 'It's alright, it's alright,' until the sound of them resonates inside you so strongly, it bursts forth from you and finds resonance throughout the world.

You are now blessed with deep tranquillity.

You are blessed with the drive to accomplish whatever you want

Look at the drive you have to get things done. According to the Taoist schema, this drive originates in your liver. Yes, that little tyrant that won't let you rest, lives under the ribs on your right side. And you have a choice. You can either run like the wind in order to keep up with its demands, or you can attempt to pacify the tyrant.

Either way, you'll need to regulate your liver energy. The best way to start that is to place a palm over the ribs on the right, take a deep breath and exhale with the sound 'shhhhhh-hhhh!', imagining your liver gently uncramping itself and expanding as if inflating like a balloon. The sound, as well as being the ancient Taoist healing sound for the liver as practiced by ancient Taoists since ancient Taoists first walked the Earth, also serves to quieten the mind. The effect of this is to draw the attention partly away from the external world and into the interior whence all power originates – a moment away from the trance of work-a-day-or-night reality – in order that you may be refreshed and renewed while in the midst of your daily and nightly doings.

You are now blessed with the drive to accomplish whatever you want.

instant enlightenment — 69

You are blessed with
invincible determination

The most important part of each day and night is determining in which mode you wish to experience the next phase of time, whether it's a minute or a year. For instance, you can choose to experience today and tonight in a relaxed state, to be content with whatever occurs because you remember that just being alive is gift enough – anything beyond is a bonus. You can choose to remember to appreciate every tiny detail of the experience of being, today and tonight. Choose to remain body-centred, because while you're alive, your body is both your temple (in which you contact the spiritual realms) and your nightclub (in which you have a damn good time).

So choose to let your focus remain centred in bodily awareness, then allow the theatre of life to unfold all around you and delight you the whole day and night long. Determine to be open to all kinds of unexpected opportunities and delights. Determine to be the bearer of all kinds of unexpected opportunities and delights for others. Above all, determine to love and be loved.

This process does something palpable to the quality of the energy coursing through you and swirling all around you – it quickens the vibratory rate.

You are now blessed with invincible determination.

instant enlightenment 70

You are blessed with the thrill of stepping out of your comfort zone

Wish for things clearly enough, visualize them manifesting with enough intent and eventually, in the fullness of time, they manifest. The shape and form of how they actually do that depends on variables beyond your control – just as with any dream (for this is all but a dream), faces and places may change, but the essence of what you want along with the feelings you want to feel as a result, will be yours (momentarily, for all is just passing form here).

But just as they do, you may feel as if the tectonic plates of your subconscious mind are moving. You may feel as if the ground beneath your metaphorical feet is amorphous. This can be uncomfortable and disquieting because by the manifestation of new situations, you are necessarily required to step outside the zone of activity you've become habituated to.

But that's only fear operating. Even if you are quaking in your boots, when you reach agreement with yourself that all change is good, then it will be. You determine the nature and quality of your experience of reality by the agreements you reach with yourself about how reality is.

So saying, say, 'All change is good!' Good! Now keep repeating it till agreement is reached and everything you wish to be made manifest, will be.

You are now blessed with the thrill of stepping out of your comfort zone.

instant enlightenment 71

You are blessed with sanity

The mind is a crazy monkey that needs constant training and supervision lest it default to the deluded mode – deluding you into believing in the reality of appearances.

Always at the core of all thoughts and experiences, behind all considerations of the mind, is the ineffable – let us call it 'Tao'. Hold to that 'Tao' deep within at all times and you'll enjoy sanity in the moment. Lose it even for one moment and you're a crazy monkey.

By the same token, there's nothing wrong with being a crazy monkey from time to time as long as you don't hurt anyone, including yourself. Every mode has its place.

Tell yourself, 'No matter how much of a crazy monkey I can be, at the core of me is sanity,' and carry on as you were.

You are now blessed with sanity.

instant enlightenment 72

You are blessed with being a being of light

Remember the importance of breathing, especially in the midst of a drama that could turn out to have a sad ending – remember to breathe, relax your body and remain centred in the present moment, without projecting into the future for even one minute, and remain in that state from moment to moment. Obviously, while you do this, you continue getting on with what you have to do, but you do so as a being of light rather than as a being of fright.

You are now blessed with being a being of light.

instant enlightenment 73

You are blessed with
steadfastness

I hold in great disdain the expression, 'Be careful of what you wish for because it might come true', just as I do, 'at the end of the day' or, 'when all's said and done' – can't bear them, such life-diminishing clichés do I find them to be.

The whole point of wishing is to get what you want, which doesn't mean it'll all be pleasant – nothing ever is – but better to get what you want than get what you don't. Nothing is ever all said and done or we'd have finished saying and doing it all aeons ago – there are no limits save the ones you impose on yourself. And which day, precisely, are we talking about, whose end will bestow divine omniscience? And what's wrong with mornings?

Nevertheless it has come very clear to me, that at the end of the day, when all's said and done, you really do have to be careful what you wish for because it really may come true.

When it does, it can be most unsettling. Even though you see manifesting before you the stuff you've been visualizing for years, there is still the fear of change, the awkwardness with the new that sometimes makes you want to run back to the familiar, less manifest state. But there is no going back. You have to be steadfast. Ironically, as soon as you relax into the strangeness and discomfort of the new, an exhilaration wells up from deep inside you that makes you want to run around shouting, 'I'm ok with strange!'

Try saying it to yourself anyway – it has a most calming, yet uplifting effect on the psyche, I find.

You are now blessed with steadfastness.

instant enlightenment 74

You are blessed with instigating something stupendous

Illusion reality into a different shape – see it differently, with enough psychic focus, and it will shift to reflect your vision. That's the basis of sorcery, so be a bit saucy and spend a few focused moments visioning, not only yourself at peace, wise, wealthy and respected in your own life, but also the world in general at peace, with enough to go round for everyone and with wisdom and respect as the prevalent ethos.

Do it even as we speak, and you will see through the dust and the earth a'rumblin', a new golden era of civilization emerging now.

It's important to have a grand goal in sight – it helps you through the dark tunnels of life, providing a 'magnet' to pull you out the other end. Wrap the vision in a frame of bright light and watch it disappear into the ether, trusting it to have an effect.

You are now blessed with instigating something stupendous.

instant enlightenment 75

You are blessed with psychic awareness

You want to be as much in command of your situation, from moment to moment, as you possibly can. That's why you want to see beneath the surface of things to the subtext, to gain insight into how the pattern of things will evolve over time, to be as prepared as possible. For this you must access your psychic ability – the ability to access your unconscious mind, which according to Taoists (both Wayward and Traditional) already knows everything in the entire universe – your brain acting as a filter, only feeding your conscious mind as much information as you need to get on with the business of day-to-day survival.

To induce a subtle yet powerful widening of that filter now (if you feel ready to process the extra flow of data it will bring), take your left forefinger and place it firmly but lovingly on your right upper arm at the tip of your deltoid (shoulder cap muscle), just where it meets your biceps, forming that cute little dimple you get when you've been working out, approximately four inches down from the tip of your right shoulder. Press firmly enough to produce a strong yet pleasant ache for up to, but no more than, 70 seconds. Repeat on the other arm. Repeat this seven times a day and within three days your telepathic, psychometric, clairvoyant, clairaudient and clairsentient awareness will have increased exponentially by an unspecified but noteworthy amount.

Then try to still the clamour of the superficial in your forebrain enough to hear the deeper messages coming from your central brain region, and learn to differentiate between the two.

You are now blessed with psychic awareness.

instant enlightenment 76

You are blessed with all-embracing, startling clarity

There's something disturbingly privileged about living through and witnessing first-hand such momentous phases of human history as the one we're in now. This will be the stuff of history lessons a hundred years from now, if there are still schools, or even people, for that matter.

The key to sanity at this and every time is to remain centred in the present. So if you find your mind projecting as is its wont, pull it back to become aware instead of the breath and consciously decelerate the tempo, deepen the movement (of the diaphragm), feel the life force in your belly and picture a clear diamond mysteriously lit from within, rotating very slowly on its own axis in the centre of your brain. Almost instantaneously you'll notice your mind become still and full of light. Then choose a mode – calm will do – by declaring, for instance, 'Today, I choose calm!' and carry on as you were.

You are now blessed with all-embracing, startling clarity.

You are blessed with being incredibly sexy

You can totally alter the way other people respond to you today and tonight by programming a thought into your circuitry through constant silent repetition, whilst in the midst of being involved in your work, rest or play.

For example if you were to repeat, 'I am incredibly sexy, desirable, attractive, magnetic, charismatic and appealing and wonderful people are drawn to me today to share the pleasure and fun of being alive!' you'd no doubt be amazed at the way things turn out.

You are now blessed with being incredibly sexy.

instant enlightenment 78

You are blessed with a run of
seamless reality

Technology, and all the comforts and ease it promises, is only a reflection of your own innate intelligence. You utilize it to make your reality as seamless as possible because you hate those awkward pauses between the lines.

So experiment when finding yourself with gaping voids in, say, the midst of a conversation and being thus thrust into pause mode – perhaps momentarily stymied by a fit of awkwardness, shyness or self-consciousness about your shoes, clothes, face or hairstyle – when you'd least like to be. Relax into the gap – surrender to the awkward moment – release into the uncomfortable cracks between the smooth action, and just breathe and feel awkward if that's what you're feeling.

You are now blessed with a run of seamless reality.

instant enlightenment 79

*You are blessed with the power
to overcome your inner loser*

Today, tonight, anything is possible. Whatever you want, you can have it. Leave the details blank – the identities of the players involved, the appearance of what you manifest, the surface effect, in other words, is not something you can control – but the essence can be determined. So if, say, you want perfect success to flow in your life over the next few months, you can have it. It won't look exactly like anything you can imagine, but it will give you exactly the experience you're looking for. Then accept it graciously when it comes.

Meantime, pick any situation that's troubling you now and dare to see the outcome you want. Then say to yourself, 'This or something even better is already in the irreversible process of manifestation,' and carry on as you were.

It's crucial to observe the negative reaction you will get to this from your inner loser, the unconscious resistance to getting what you want – focussing on all the things that could go wrong, all the hassles you could have. Assure your inner loser that you have its best interest at heart. Then say boldly and confidently, yet modestly and graciously, 'Today, tonight, anything is possible – whatever I want, I can have it.' And it will be so.

You are now blessed with the power to overcome your inner loser.

instant enlightenment 80

You are blessed with dexterity

Look at your hands and think of all the things they've done in your life so far – all the washing of dishes, the scrubbing of surfaces, the typing of words, the caressing, the gesticulating, the turning of steering wheels, the changing of gears, the grabbing of objects, the carrying of luggage, the opening of doors, the dialing of numbers, the pushing of buttons, the forming of fists, yes, even the stimulation of sexual organs and all the other near infinite number of actions those hands have made. Let them remind you of the miracle of your existence. It's important to remind yourself of that as regularly and often as you can because it's all too easy to forget, lost in the hustle, bustle and stress of the everyday.

Remembering your own miraculousness is a major key to enlightenment. If you manage to get a clear view of your hands up close, while dreaming, you can take command of the dream. Waking life, walking in the world of the ten thousand things, is no less of a dream. So contemplate your hands and take command of your life.

You are now blessed with dexterity.

instant enlightenment — 81

You are blessed with divine patience

From the divine perspective of the all-seeing, all-knowing eye (or I) within you, this is all theatre – you, your life, the people in your life, me, these words – and time and space are merely theatrical devices to prevent everything happening to you at once in one spot, thus causing a solid mass of condensed wreckage with you at its core. That doesn't mean you mustn't honour it, however. On the contrary, you must always honour the play and give it the space and time it takes to unfold of itself, or it ceases to be enjoyable for you and everyone else involved.

Honour the illusion of the divine theatre, but desist from colluding with others who wish to lose themselves so much in the charade they forget their own divine nature, and begin to believe they are the roles they play to the extent they become impatient and stressed as a result.

Draw breath deeply and say, 'I now freely desist from colluding with those who wish to lose themselves in the charade of life, while honouring the illusion to the full'.

Now wait three minutes as a gesture of patience while a moment of enlightenment engulfs you.

You are now blessed with divine patience.

instant enlightenment 82

You are blessed with compassion for your own vulnerability

The fragility of your existence, your vulnerability, can only be greeted with compassion. But to achieve this state of being it is prerequisite to draw your awareness back into the centre of your brain, far away from the world of the ten thousand things, relax your chest so your human warmth can flow more freely, and breathe from deep inside your belly, so the force of life can surge through you.

Everything in your view can now clearly be seen as nothing more, or less, than a swirl of dancing atoms – events arising from the nothingness of non-existence that underscores existence and returning thence once they've done their turn and received their due applause or hurled tomatoes. The poignancy of their coming and going – of your coming and going and of the coming and going of everyone in your life – touches somewhere in your heart that makes you want to cry.

You are now blessed with compassion for your own vulnerability.

instant enlightenment 83

*You are blessed with
enlightenment*

The Taoist concept of the dance of yin and yang – dark and light, stillness and action, taking and giving, being entertained and entertaining, weak and strong, soft and hard; the two eternally balancing and counterbalancing on every level in every dimension and aspect of your life – though extremely simple is utterly profound, and without any shadow of a doubt provides a major key to enlightenment here and now, even as you sit reading this.

You have grown up in a world in which your education, based on the old-school Cartesian model, has taught you to prefer this over that and that over this. Hence dark becomes bad and light good; stillness becomes bad and action good; taking becomes bad and giving good and so on – and of course vice versa depending on the situation. You have been trained in the either/or model of reality.

Instead, simply notice whichever phase is occurring with regards your current sphere of attention, be willing to suspend judgement, be content to remain in the observer's position, no longer preferring one phase of being over another. Thus stillness becomes both good *and* bad, action becomes both good *and* bad and so on, until both good and bad themselves become both good and bad and ultimately cancel each other out, and you are enlightened.

You are now blessed with enlightenment.

You are blessed with the capacity for exquisite pleasure

Whatever happens to you, however horrible, happens because, at the deepest level of being, you tell it to. You are responsible. While you may baulk at such a notion, the key to its veracity lies in the words, 'at the deepest level of your being'.

By the same token, at the deepest level of being, you are also free to tell wonderful things to happen.

But this level of being, access to which grants you the power to actually shape your reality, is not the local level. It's the universal level beyond the illusory constraints of linear time, on which your being is synonymous with the Tao, or universal being, itself.

Gain access to it now by being meditative and saying, 'I now access that deepest layer of self and recreate my reality to suit me better', and your deepest self will cause you such exquisite sublime pleasure, your every thought will be bathed in light.

You are now blessed with the capacity for exquisite pleasure.

instant enlightenment 85

You are blessed with rapture

Next time you step out in public and find yourself in a crowded place, let go of your chest – release all the holding on in there and allow it to relax fully. Align your spinal column, more or less, allowing it to be as perpendicular to the ground as you can manage, breathe quite slowly and deeply, let go of the habitual agenda in your head and, above all, desist from negatively judging or, in any way, limiting the potential magnificence of those around you. Then allow your love to flow to one and all and you may well find yourself in a state of rapture, a state of not only being one with the entirety of creation, but also two, three and even ten thousandfold with it, and all of you dancing together as one on the head of a pin.

You are now blessed with rapture.

instant enlightenment —— 86

You are blessed with perfect
speed

When the outside, yang, is moving at a furious pace let the inside, yin, move very slowly as a counterbalance.

Focus on slowing yourself down internally by decelerating your breathing pace whilst in the midst of extreme outer activity, and you'll function far more effectively and enjoy the whole thing far more as a result.

You can supplement this with repetition of a little affirmative ditty such as, 'The more slowly I go, the faster I get where I'm going.'

You are now blessed with perfect speed.

instant enlightenment 87

You are blessed with life
progressing with immense
elegance

You're suffering the delays and glitches of life with forbearance but it's still pissing you off – you feel miffed that life would dare to act with such inelegance in your presence – how dare it!

So you step back and imagine the natural warmth, goodness and love in your heart now radiating outwards in ever-expanding circles until it connects you to every living being in the entire universe.

And as you do, you trigger a movement of energy and not only will your day and night be filled with great ease and enjoyment, but everything you want to happen will happen with immense elegance.

You are now blessed with life progressing with immense elegance.

instant enlightenment 88

You are blessed with full
realization of your potential

Dream of the life you want to be living now. Hold onto the vision against all the odds, and in the face of almost constant adversity and, eventually, almost as if by magic (notwithstanding all the work that goes into it), it will manifest itself before your very eyes. In case you may be doubting your own dream, this is to encourage you to hold to the vision, have faith, be perseverant, do the work required and, above all, take the risks involved to make your adventure as huge as it can possibly be. Not that it will always make you feel happy, but if you only have one innings in your present form, why spend it holed up in the cul-de-sac of life?

You are now blessed with full realization of your potential.

instant enlightenment 89

You are blessed with reason to celebrate

It is imperative not to get lost in the trance of the ten thousand things now. Instead, do something to strengthen your body and spiritual connection. Do some of your favourite kind of exercise. Sit and have some moments of stillness and silence. Remain alert, awake and above all collected. Resist going into denial about the state of affairs you're in. Instead, welcome it as the adventure movie it is and prepare to enjoy it, no matter how grisly the action becomes.

It's the only way – embrace reality like a warrior. This doesn't preclude celebration; far from it. Celebrate every precious minute – this one in particular. But don't base your celebration on the idea of things remaining as they are. We've entered a time of overwhelming unpredictability. The only sure thing you can predict is utter change on every level.

Let that fuel your pleasure in this and every moment with the people you love and above all yourself. And keep breathing. One way or another, it'll all work out fine.

You are now blessed with reason to celebrate.

instant enlightenment 90

You are blessed with

integration

With all the great strides forward you've made in your life, you're still feeling somehow constricted, dammit. Crawl about on the floor. Soften your body. Get up and dance. Pull silly faces. Talk gibberish – in short, do whatever it takes to make contact with the childlike realm. Then relax, sit quietly and examine the fears of your own small child within and check whether, how, or how much they're driving or inhibiting you.

Simply noticing, without making negative judgement, is enough to make the child feel acknowledged and thus safe to release its grip. It also doesn't hurt to see yourself taking him, or her, by the hand and going out for a walk, upon which you have a serious but loving heart-to-heart chat together. Ask that you may be free of all self-limitations self-imposed unconsciously by your wounded inner child, that you may soar and fly through your day and night as a self-determining warrior with full authority over your life. And you will be.

You are now blessed with integration.

instant enlightenment — 91

You are blessed with equipoise

The trick to achieving equipoise in the face of internal and external upheaval is to accommodate the swing within and around you. To sit with it all comfortably in your belly, like a Buddha digesting a well-rounded, finely prepared dish of sweet and sour chicken (or tofu, if of course you're vegetarian or a chicken-loather).

This requires the courage to allow yourself an appreciation for the thrill of the meeting of apparent opposites, for the encompassing of extremes. Yes, it's the time to be courageous, to be a warrior and a hero, but not in isolation – it's time to stop thinking about yourself solely as an individual and to reach out and extend your love, help and kindness to everyone you can. Because the only force that ultimately overcomes everything – economic cycles, geopolitical shifts, ecological turbulence, as well as inner confusion, fear, stymiedness and all the rest of your own and others' existential mayhem – is love.

You are now blessed with equipoise.

instant enlightenment 92

You are blessed with revelation

Practise awareness of the divine presence now, not just in your soul, heart and mind, where it is relatively easy to feel, but all around you, in every situation, every action, every person, every mammal, bird, fish, reptile, spider, insect, plant, weed, flower, twig, blade of grass, tree, forest, river, ocean, lake, swimming pool, fishpond, mountain, rock, pebble, waterfall, toilet flush, perfume bottle, tea bag, windowpane, cloud, shoe, dance and what-have-you, that populates your external reality.

You can see it as the Great Spirit if you're in a Native American sort of mood, as the Tao if you're in a Taoist sort of mood, or as the primordial, meta-conscious, generative force underlying, containing and animating all of existence and non-existence, if you're in whatever sort of mood that is. It really doesn't matter, as long as you train yourself to see everyone and everything not just as objects, but imbued with it.

Of course, you don't even have to do that – it's only a suggestion, but if you do follow it, whether flickeringly or concentratedly throughout the day and night, you'll enjoy some immensely insightful, revealing and altogether nourishing moments.

You are now blessed with revelation.

instant enlightenment 93

You are blessed with freedom
from addiction (if you want it)

Breathing in reinforces your core strength, breathing out connects your core to the outside. At first it feels strange – the mind wants to lose itself in distraction – but with patient repetition, awareness of the breath takes over, and your perspective begins to shift as the enlightened self, your immortal spirit body, takes command.

It is from this state that the Tao, or Great Way, starts responding by causing things to manifest in the most surprisingly elegant manner. The danger then, of course, is that you get lost in that elegance and completely forget your core, at which the Tao stops manifesting elegantly and you become despondent, resorting to such diversions as sex, drugs and shopping in a vain attempt to allay the existential unrest. However this can be precluded from the menu altogether by remembering to focus on the breathing – or if you like, you can lose yourself in sex, drugs and shopping, while maintaining the core of your attention on the breathing and thus spiritualize the experience – and you will be filled with the power of pure being throughout the day and night, all your doings will be virtuous and bring you and those with whom you interact in thought, word and deed, immense and sublime joy.

You are now blessed with freedom from addiction (if you want it).

instant enlightenment 94

You are blessed with a life
without flinching

Within you is a level of consciousness on which you are aware of all the pain and suffering in the world. The normal tendency is to distract yourself from it, in an attempt to remain happy in your own life; however, it works far better if you allow yourself to feel the pain inside rather than ignore it, though not in such a way as to become maudlin.

Indeed, awareness of true joy can only exist alongside awareness of true pain. If you were to map the two onto your physical form, you'd generally find the pain in your solar plexus (upper abdomen) and the joy in your chest (heart centre). The trick is to be in all your body at once, breathing steadily, accommodating both the pain and the joy simultaneously. The key to your sanity is the steady breathing.

You are now blessed with a life without flinching.

instant enlightenment 95

You are blessed with the
capacity to accommodate even
the fear beneath all fears

Being alive can be a scary business at times, especially when everything feels back to front. Instigate a process now to regulate your energy and calm your fears by first becoming aware of what you're doing with your body, then wherever you feel yourself gripping without good reason, let go. If you're bending forwards, backwards or to the side for no reason, gently straighten yourself. If your breathing tempo is fast, slow it down and make the in-breath and out-breath of equal duration. Allow the muscles of your face to soften and relax until you're wearing an expression of utmost simplicity, if wearing any expression at all. Then relax your chest, your belly, your hips, the muscle between your legs, your thighs, your neck, and do all this as you continue to read.

Then take a brief look within at the fear beneath all fears – the fear of painful dissolution – and instead of running from it, relax into it. It's not easy, but as you continue to breathe, you manage moments of transpersonal perspective, when you're no longer taking your own particular spin on the great wheel of life and death quite so personally – you feel yourself, instead, part of an eternal continuum.

It doesn't last long and you return to yourself suddenly as if having been thrust forth from a great depth, but you notice your fear levels have dropped significantly – in fact, they've been transformed altogether into waves of excitement for simply being here.

You are now blessed with the capacity to accommodate even the fear beneath all fears.

instant enlightenment 96

You are blessed with the
capacity for great sensual
delight

Visualize yourself as a hollow bamboo standing vertically beneath a magnificent waterfall whose warm, soothing, healing, life-giving waters are even now pouring down through the top of your head and washing all tension, anxiety, doubt, self-limiting beliefs, illness, darkness and all other forms of negativity downwards and out through the opening where the soles of your feet would be, until you feel so clean, pure, warm, healed, soothed, vibrant, optimistic, confident, courageous, emboldened and fortified, you hardly know what to do with yourself.

But whatever it is you do, may it be damn sexy no matter what and let it warm you and all those with whom you interact, with great sensual and sublime delight.

You are now blessed with the capacity for great sensual delight.

instant enlightenment 97

You are blessed with sweet stillness

A certain sweetness can be accessed in the soul – your soul and the soul of the Earth – but you have to be very still to feel it. Let yourself feel that stillness now and the sweetness that comes with it, to fuel you all the way from now to infinity.

Choose it for yourself (if you want), by saying over and over,

'I love this sweet stillness.'

Then it's a simple matter of welcoming your destiny, so that whatever's happening around you, whatever comes to pass, you say, 'I love this.'

You are now blessed with sweet stillness.

instant enlightenment 98

You are blessed with feeling
altogether better than you
have in ages

A new moment, a new start, but what are you choosing to leave behind you to lighten your load on the road? Are you letting go of all the restraints on your person you can – these of course, all ones you've placed on yourself?

And while it would be tempting to list all the myriad ways you've been restricting yourself from achieving full expression, it would be far more expedient and instant, in terms of lightening your load, to focus instead on the breath and your physical posture. For here, in this moment, you have a choice to hang on to all your self-restrictive tendencies, which have, over time, embedded themselves in the soft tissue of your body, gradually hardening it till it causes your skeletal structure to become misaligned, or to release them.

The way to release is through breathing freely, paying special attention to the out-breath, so that every time you exhale, you tell yourself you're expelling all unnecessary tension (holding on), from your mind, body and soul of the past. Then as you inhale again, tell yourself you're drawing in the very essence of self-liberation as you welcome this new moment into your life.

Repeat at least three full breath cycles and carry on, as you were, now feeling far more optimistic, powerful, beautiful and altogether better than you have in ages.

You are now blessed with feeling altogether better than you have in ages.

You are blessed with the warmth of a compassionate Buddha

Amazing things happen now as you connect to others from the heart. Without being intrusive, look deeply into the eyes of people you meet today or tonight and, keeping your chest relaxed, allow your natural warmth to flow to them as you interact.

To amplify the effects of this flow, press firmly into the 'Compassionate Buddha' points in the dead centre of each palm until they ache pleasantly, and you will no doubt be equally pleasantly surprised by the levels of warmth and connectedness that fill your day and night.

You are now blessed with the warmth of a compassionate Buddha.

instant enlightenment 100

You are blessed with true magnificence

When you worry about your life, and the lives of those you love, being at the mercy of the possible greedy, shortsighted, small-minded actions of apparent lunatics, remember that worry carries negative energy to its object, thus increasing the potential for negative results.

Choose instead to see the spirit of human magnificence reign supreme in the world of affairs, so that rash moves by everyone – from world leaders and all those with temporal power, to the person on the street – may be avoided at this time, thus preventing what otherwise could so easily develop into unspeakable bloodshed and horror. See a softening occur deep in the chest of every human being now as the spirit enters and an era of wisdom, tolerance, liberty and abundance for everybody ensues – for as you see it, if you see it clearly enough, so will it be.

You are now blessed with true magnificence.

instant enlightenment 101

You are blessed with Heaven on Earth

See all the people to the north, to the south, to the east and to the west of you, in a state of deep peace. See a wave of calm tolerance pervade everywhere. See people everywhere suddenly realize that fighting and dominating each other is no longer the way forward. See people everywhere cooperating to ensure not only our survival but our prosperity and abundance too. See us all connected at the level of deepest self now.

Yes, it can happen.

You are now blessed with Heaven on Earth.

instant enlightenment 102

You are blessed with the splendour, power and glory of your own true self

Keep breathing now, breathing freely without ever holding your breath for a moment, except of course when under water or under attack of poison gas or suchlike.

It's really all as simple and straightforward as that, life – just keep breathing.

Too fundamental? Too basic for you? There is no greater key to peace of mind and self-mastery in the moment at your disposal than the taking command of the style and manner of your breathing patterns. Slow your breath: slow your mind. Make your breath smooth: your thinking will be also. Calm your breathing: calm yourself. And let every breath bring you closer to the splendour, power and glory of the Tao, at the core of your own true self.

You are now blessed with the splendour, power and glory of your own true self.

instant enlightenment 103

You are blessed with perfect dignity

A healthy balance between driving yourself to get done what you want, or need, to get done and remembering your own mortality, hence the futility of chasing the details of life, is desirable now, lest you run yourself into the ground.

The key to achieving this balance is in the breathing. Paying attention to your breathing and allowing it to be at the core of your experience, no matter what else you're doing, immediately shifts the dynamic between being and doing. The power to do arises from the power of being. Allow the root of your attention to remain on the breath, the trunk of your attention to remain in your spinal column, and the branches of your awareness to extend out into the world of the ten thousand things, as you go about your business.

Visualize yourself now as that tree, with your roots going deep into the ground beneath you, your trunk lengthening towards the sky and the sap rising and extending through your branches all the way to your fingertips. Then, rather than you chasing the world of the ten thousand things, wait, like any good tree would, for the world of the ten thousand things to come to you.

But don't think about it – just breathe and let it happen.

You are now blessed with perfect dignity.

instant enlightenment 104

You are blessed with connectedness

You're feeling cut-off, alone, worthless, unlovable and it's perturbing you.

But there is a level on which you're fully connected to all the warmth and love in the universe – and you can find it within you right now if you want, simply by believing it's there and saying hello.

Feel that connection between us, of spirit talking directly to spirit, where fundamentally, though it may appear there are over six billion individual human beings on the planet, there is at the core of things, only one – you – me – the Tao – or whatever you want to call it, and in feeling it, you all at once experience a rush of life-force that fuels you through the day and night and makes your spirit feel extremely large and all-embracing now.

You are now blessed with connectedness.

instant enlightenment 105

You are blessed with trust

It's always been a shaky thing, this business of trusting other people. Far better to learn to trust yourself. Once you trust yourself, others tend to trust you too, which in turn enables you to trust them back, but it all begins inside you.

And what you can trust yourself to be, and hence others to be in return, is human – fully human, with all the divinely complex magnificence and deeply convoluted mess that implies. Nothing more, nothing less.

You can start the process simply by repeating, 'I trust myself' over and over until you mean it, or you can just trust yourself to trust yourself and get on with the day.

And talking of getting on with your day, let yours be a fine one now, full of many happy surprises, mutual trust and bonhomie with your fellow humans – your night too.

You are now blessed with trust.

instant enlightenment 106

You are blessed with courage

It requires great courage to surrender to change. Courage to allow yourself to keep going in a forward direction even while quaking tremulously in your boots.

Courage is not something you're born with or not. Courage is an *a priori* quality available to anyone anytime who cares to access it, which is done simply by saying, 'I choose to access courage now'. You can augment the effect by pressing firmly on the underside of your wrist, at the base of the palm in line with the little finger. This is a point called 'the spirit door', lying on the heart meridian, useful to calm the nerves and stimulate the flow of heart energy or courage.

Additionally, adjust your stance towards change in general, so that instead of automatically seeing change as bad, choose to see it as good, no matter what. To help this along and as a simple experiment with reality, train yourself to welcome all new information – including the extra tasks and new responsibilities that land on your plate daily and nightly – with an 'oh, yes!' instead of the usual 'oh, no!' you tend to default to as a rule, without noticing.

You are now blessed with courage.

instant enlightenment 107

You are blessed with quite a life

What else can I tell you? Nothing much, other than that if you notice yourself giving yourself a hard time at any time during the day or night, stop immediately. Blow the air out of your lungs, take in a new lungful and say to yourself, in the manner of a loving parent to a child it adores, and for whom it can do no wrong, 'I love you so much I could eat you!' Then carry on as you were (but without giving yourself a hard time for it anymore – there's enough hardship in the world without you adding to it unnecessarily).

May you receive many unexpected delights, magnificent surprises, that thrill you to the quick every day and night of your life from now on. And every night, as your head hits the pillow and sleep overcomes you, may your last thought be, 'This is quite a life!'

You are now blessed with quite a life.

instant enlightenment 108

You are blessed with seeing the joke

See the joke
of attempting to poke
at the cloak
of the Tao.
It's a mysterious affair
and to glimpse it is rare,
even if you've trained just like the Bare …
Foot.
Put …
your mind in your belly,
stop watching the telly
and drop all those thoughts
that are nasty or smelly.
Breathe with ease,
relax your knees
and if you're lucky,
you'll feel the breeze
(of the Tao).
Now.

You are now blessed with seeing the joke.

(Thank you)

end of transmission

Return of the Urban Warrior

High-speed spirituality for people on the run

Barefoot Doctor takes you on a high-speed spiritual trip, with potent doses of humour and demystified Taoist philosophy, containing (almost) everything you need to know to excel in the fast and furious twenty-first century without cracking up. Includes:

- Advanced Taoist meditation and self-healing techniques for beginners and old hands alike
- Contemporary urban Taoist life skills to help you 'spiritualize' even the dullest moments and be the slickest operator on the block
- The ancient Taoist 'warrior wisdom' programme for peace, prosperity and peak performance installed into your circuitry simply through reading (this text)

The original barefoot doctors travelled the ancient Orient, healing people and lifting their spirits. This is the twenty-first century urban version.

Liberation

The perfect holistic antidote to stress, depression and other unhealthy states of mind

> Freedom is found within. Your shackles are your own inner struggle – your angst and anguish, your worries about money, your frustrations, your greed, your self-limiting thoughts and your fears keep you from being free. But if you're willing to take a chance, to go out on a limb and download this text onto your inner hard drive, you hold the key to liberation in your hand.

As always, Barefoot Doctor offers the full prescription: Taoist healing methods and philosophy, with an added pinch of Hinduism, Buddhism, Shamanism, Humanism and a heavy smattering of timeless Basic Commonsensism. Barefoot's remedies provide the perfect antidote to depression, deprivation, fear, loneliness, shyness, grief, grudges and all the other unhelpful mind-states life in the post-modern urban spin-cycle throws up.

Twisted Fables for Twisted Minds

This will either heal you or make you go insane

Leave all your troubles behind and come with Barefoot Doctor and a host of unlikely but loveable characters on a psychedelic transglobal quest involving heists, twisted plots, sex, drugs, mystical mayhem, the meaning of life and cosmic consciousness. Barefoot Doctor – or is it an angel? – pops up throughout to inject the story with his unique brand of Taoist wisdom.

Barefoot Doctor's opening salvo into the world of fiction is an exciting narrative fable, delivered with all the eloquence, wit and merriment you've come to expect from his writing. So if you've ever struggled to make sense of life, been bruised by the ups and downs of it all, found it hard to keep your mind clear in the midst of a crazy world, or simply craved some solace, this is the book for you.

Manifesto

The Internal Revolution

- Want more money/wealth?
- Want more love/sex?
- Want a new job/career?
- Want boundless health, energy and radiant beauty?
- Want to find your true path through the maze of modern life and reach your goal of full self-expression so you can live long and prosper?

Manifesto shows you how to get exactly what you want out of life, with ancient Taoist visualization, positive thinking and relaxation techniques made simple and clear, backed up by sound, practical Taoist philosophies and attitudes to encourage and help you keep it all in perspective as you go.

'Funny, wise and provocative.' *Sunday People*

S P E C I A L   O F F E R

Order these selected Thorsons and Element titles direct from the publisher and receive £1 off each title! Visit www.thorsonselement.com for additional special offers.

Free post and packaging for UK delivery (overseas and Ireland, £2.00 per book).

Manifesto Barefoot Doctor (0-00-716486-6)	£12.00 - £1.00 = £11.00
Liberation Barefoot Doctor (0-00-716510-2)	£7.99 - £1.00 = £6.99
Return of the Urban Warrior Barefoot Doctor (0-00-712297-7)	£14.99 - £1.00 = £13.99
Twisted Fables for Twisted Minds Barefoot Doctor (0-00-716485-8)	£12.00 - £1.00 = £11.00

Place your order by post, phone, fax, or email, listed below. Be certain to quote reference code **713J** to take advantage of this special offer.

Mail Order Dept. (REF: **713J**)
HarperCollins*Publishers*
Westerhill Road
Bishopbriggs G64 2QT

Email: customerservices@harpercollins.co.uk
Phone: 0870 787 1724
Fax: 0870 787 1725

Credit cards and cheques are accepted. Do not send cash. Prices shown above were correct at time of press. Prices and availability are subject to change without notice.

BLOCK CAPITALS PLEASE

Name of cardholder _____
Address of cardholder _____
_____
_____

Postcode _____

Delivery address (if different) _____
_____
_____

Postcode _____

I've enclosed a cheque for £_____, made payable to HarperCollins*Publishers*, or please charge my Visa/MasterCard/Switch (circle as appropriate)

Card Number: _____
Expires: __/__   Issue No: __/__   Start Date: __/__
Switch cards need an issue number or start date validation.

thorsons element

Signature:_____

Make
www.thorsonselement.com
your online sanctuary

Get online information, inspiration and
guidance to help you on the path to physical
and spiritual well-being. Drawing on the integrity
and vision of our authors and titles, and with
health advice, articles, astrology, tarot, a
meditation zone, author interviews and events
listings, www.thorsonselement.com is a great
alternative to help create space and peace
in our lives.

So if you've always wondered about practising
yoga, following an allergy-free diet, using the
tarot or getting a life coach, we can point you
in the right direction.

thorsons
element